This book is dedicated to all the animals that have touched my life and taught me so much about the wonders and diversity of nature.

ABOUT THE AUTHOR

Joel Rosenthal grew up in apartments in Washington D.C. For decades he worked as a biologist in the Washington metropolitan area.

In 2000 he established Point of View Farm, Inc., a 501 (C) (3) non-profit animal sanctuary, and began operations in West Virginia. His goal was to care for injured and orphaned animals so that they could be released, or be provided with a permanent home.

In 2005 he was charged with the crime of illegally possessing wildlife, a week old fawn. Over the next four years he, without any legal experience or help, fought the State asserting that he had a legal right to his activities.

His odyssey demonstrates how fragile and marginal our legal system can be, yet how justice can be achieved by a dogged persistence.

After dozens of court appearances from Magistrate Court through the West Virginia Supreme Court of Appeals to the U. S. Federal District Court, he prevailed.

This book should inspire anyone who feels he/she has been unjustly accused of a crime, anyone in the legal profession and those who care about animals.

Rosenthal, Joel
    Bambi and the Supremes
    1st Edition
    p. cm.
    preassigned Library of Congress Control Number: 2012904153
    ISBN 978-0-9853277-0-5
    1. Justice. 2. Law. 3. Animals. 4. Courts. 5. Rosenthal, Joel. 6. Title

The Cover Picture was taken of the author standing in front of the West Virginia
    Supreme Court of Appeals building, following his Hearing.
    All other photos were taken by the author

Printed in the United States of America

Bambi and the Supremes

By Joel Rosenthal

MY FIGHT FOR
THE ANIMALS

I LIVED IN THIS CABIN ON POINT OF VIEW FARM

ACKNOWLEDGMENTS

Two judges have my undying respect and appreciation for their ability to decipher and apply the law.

First there is the Honorable, Joseph C. Pomponio, Jr., Judge Circuit Court, Pocahontas County, West Virginia. Judge Pomponio was able to see through the nonsense put forth by the State of West Virginia. He read, understood and applied, faithfully the laws as written and made a courageous, Solomon like ruling.

The second is the Honorable John Preston Bailey, Chief U.S. District Judge, West Virginia. Judge Bailey like Judge Pomponio focused on the issues at hand and how they legally applied to my lawsuit.

I would also like to thank John Leyzorek, a Pocahontas County friend, who untiringly read all the postings of the courts, read all my responses, listened to all my ranting and ravings, attended all the court proceedings and rendered to me wise thoughts and insights.

My gratitude is also extended to Drew Tanner, reporter for the Pocahontas Times. Misdemeanor cases normally receive only a footnote in the newspaper. Drew attended all the trials including the Hearing at the Supreme Court in Charleston. His public coverage of my case helped to bolster and further my cause.

And of course I would like to thank all my friends who attended court hearings and trials and offered their support.

In a weird sort of way I also want to thank everyone in the judicial and prosecutorial system of West Virginia who made it their mission to distort and prevaricate about the facts, to conduct themselves in an illegal manner and to demonstrate how thin a veneer is this concept we call democracy. My journey to learn and navigate through the legal system could not have happened had they acted responsibly from the beginning.

I would also like to thank Robert Higdon, a former friend and a defense attorney, who condemned my actions and my desires to fight the system. Bob refused to counsel me on even the basics and urged me to simply plead guilty. This inspired me to be more determined to not only defend myself, but to demonstrate that I was a far better lawyer then he.

Finally I would like to thank Colleen Flannery and Linda Silvern for the long hours they contributed towards editing; consulting and helping me put together this book.

TABLE OF CONTENTS

PREFACE

Justice in the United States is guaranteed in many ways, but the realization of this justice sometimes can require a long, arduous and very problematic path.

Almost all of us have come in contact at one time or another with the "criminal justice system." A parking ticket or a vehicle moving violation is the extent of this contact for most of us. All are misdemeanors. And for most of us the ignominy of receiving such a citation weighs heavily until we pay the fine. In many cases we feel the citation is not justified, but because of commitments, the time and money involved we simply pay the ticket in order to get on with our lives as soon as possible.

Occasionally, if we feel violated some of us will go to court to fight our case and indeed many citizens do win these cases. Anyone in this position knows, understands and feels that satisfaction of such a victory.

And then every once in a while there is a set of circumstances whereby no matter how minor the accusation a principle and way of life conflict with the authorities. In such an instance fighting the accusation no matter the consequences becomes a necessity. Most in this situation would turn to professional legal representation. And for most this is the wisest course. For myself, though, I was determined to learn about the law and how it works as much as I wanted my case to set a precedent. Such a circumstance is chronicled in these pages.

In a crazy sort of way I have to thank almost everyone involved in the justice system in the Pocahontas County Courthouse in West Virginia.

INTRODUCTION

Never in a million years would I have ever thought that someday I would be defending a judge against the State of West Virginia in front of the State Supreme Court.

I am not a lawyer and never knew anything about the criminal justice system other than paying a few citations for vehicle violations.

At 63 years of age I was living the very first dream I can remember having as a child when this legal saga began.

When I was four years old my folks began taking me to a farm owned by former neighbors of our apartment complex in Washington D. C. It was then that I knew I wanted someday to have a farm and take care of animals.

After a career in science and a period for travel I found myself in the financial situation whereby this dream of having my farm could come true. So at the age of 58 I planned out the hows and wheres.

Wanting to be able to make a difference I decided that establishing a non-profit charitable organization that could buy the property and act to improve the environment, aid wildlife and engage in educational programs would be the most balanced course of action.

When I was about 12 years old my younger sister had a book called "It Looks Like This, A Point of View Book." It was a book of animal drawings showing each animal from a different point of view. It was then that I decided to name my place "Point of View Farm."

Having grown up in the Mid-Atlantic States, my first choice for the farm location focused on this region. New England and the Pacific Northwest were also considered. My love, however, for the soft mountains of West Virginia continually brought me to this area to find my farm.

Finally, after searching for a few years I found on the internet what turned out to be the perfect place for me. Located in the heart of the Allegheny Mountains in Pocahontas County, West Virginia this 262 acre tract had a log cabin and a couple of run in sheds. Most of the farm was tucked into Calvin Price State Forest and its 10,000 acres. The only access to this land was via a 450 foot drive through the Greenbrier River. No other roads reached the farm and no one else lived on this side of the river for miles. Another bonus was that the farm came with an eight acre island in the river. A pristine mountain stream, Oldham Run, bisected the farm.

And best of all was that the farm contained almost every ecological niche available in West Virginia. Not only are beautiful meadows and fields sculptured over millions of years by the river undulated over most of the property, but a whole mountainside rose on the eastern border. Low land forests blended with those of the mountaintops. A huge wetland contained a rhododendron forest so dense it seemed one could live beneath its canopy. Oldham Run even cut through a canyon.

For me this was the perfect place to have a sanctuary where I could engage in animal rehabilitation and be isolated so as not to interfere with others nor have them interfere with me.

Settlement for the purchase of the property occurred on July 3, 2000.

Chapter 1

GOING TO WEST VIRGINIA

West Virginia sits along the Appalachian Mountains in the Mid-Atlantic States. It is a land locked state that was created by carving it out of a portion of Virginia in 1863. It became a key border state during the U.S. Civil War. While most of the state lies south of the Mason-Dixon Line a portion, the northern panhandle is north of this line and occupies a small sliver between Pennsylvania and Ohio. It is the only state to be encompassed entirely by the Appalachian Regional Commission.

The population of about 1.8 million residents or 75 persons per square mile is relatively steady.

With an average attitude of about 1500 feet the state boasts the highest average altitude of any state east of the Mississippi River. Hence it is called the mountain state. There are 55 counties, but those counties in the eastern central part of the state contain the backbone of the mountains.

Pocahontas County borders the State of Virginia and is central to the state from a north south perspective. The county with approximately one thousand square miles is one of the largest in the state, but has less than nine thousand residents or about 9 per square mile. Sixty percent of the county is owned by government agencies. Marlinton is the county seat with a population of about 1000. Several other towns comprise another couple of thousand people, leaving most of the countryside sparsely populated. This county is emblematic of West Virginia being called "Wild and Wonderful." Pocahontas County has the highest average altitude of any county east of the Mississippi River and is the birthplace for 8 rivers in West Virginia. The largest river, the Greenbrier River begins in the northern part of the county and runs south through the entire county.

Natural resources are the focus of almost all of the state's revenues. Coal, oil, gas and timber are harvested on a large scale. Hiking, biking, camping, fishing and hunting make up the bulk of the rest. Pocahontas County has very little mining and its timber harvests are diminished from just a couple of decades ago. Pocahontas County continues to lose population due to a lack of jobs and its rural location. At one time three high schools served the county, now there is only one. The entire school population is only about 1300 students.

Economically the entire state has always ranked at the lower end of income per household for all the states. And concomitantly the standard of living for West Virginians has been low. Any state whose natural resources are exploited by outsiders and where the infrastructure cannot handle lots of innovation or business immigration will always have a population with substandard opportunities.

I live in one of the more rural and remote areas of the county. At the southern end of the county the Greenbrier River flows at about 2,000 ft. elevation. Through an undeveloped area six miles outside of Hillsboro the river meanders along the east side of what is now an 80 mile hiking/biking trail that used to be a spur of the C & O railroad when lumber was king. The tracks are gone now. A narrow asphalt road (Beard Rd.) provides access to the trail and to my dirt right of way between the trail and the river.

Following the river south for about a third of a mile the dirt road simply drops right down the steep bank and into the river. This is at one of the widest points on the river and by looking 450 feet across one can see the driveway to Point of View Farm, Inc., my non-profit charitable organization. Driving through the river is the only access to the property. Fortunately, the river bottom is covered with a layer of rock. However, if the river is running more than just a couple of feet deep, no one can drive across.

Fording the river to my driveway, I pass just upstream of an eight acre island which is part of the farm.

The farm consists of 262 acres of wonderful meadows and fields, forests and mountains sides. One border of the farm is against the river and the other is contiguous with Calvin Price State Forest, an almost inaccessible totally mountainous land consisting of about 10,000 acres. The state forest has no improved recreational areas, no homes or buildings, no agriculture, no mining and only a limited amount of timbering. Hunting is allowed, but access is very difficult in those areas bordering me. Point of View Farm has no adjacent private property owners. A few private areas with hunting cabins do exist further up river, but nobody but me lives on "my" side of the river for miles. Upstream several miles and adjacent to Calvin Price State Forest to the north is Watoga State Park where there are recreational amenities for human comfort.

A pristine mountain stream, Oldham Run, which has its origin in Calvin Price State Forest, bisects Point of View Farm. The water is drinkable. Several springs begin on the property and one used to serve a log cabin at the base of the mountain.

A "wetland" of about ten acres at the base of the mountains grows what the state forester has told me is the best pin oak forest in West Virginia. A rhododendron "forest" of several acres so thick one could live under its canopy lies between the base of the mountain and the wetland. Spectacular views of Droop Mountain rising 3700 feet above sea level to the west can be had from anywhere on the farm.

Geologically, the farm is composed mostly of an old river flood plain. Some of the fields are almost totally devoid of rock and consist of topsoil over various clays. In other sections there is a more small rock base overlain with topsoil or forest. The mountain side is rocky with boulders and is tree covered. A switchback hiking trail goes to the top of the mountain courtesy of selective logging about 25 years ago.

Vegetation varies widely. Meadow grasses and wildflowers inhabit the fields which are left fallow and not cultivated for any cash crops. Mowing is done sparingly so as not to disturb the wildlife, but multiflora rose and autumn olive, two scourge, invasive plants are mowed to the ground each year. Along the river and streams are stands of sycamore and maple and buckeye. Shagbark hickory grows in patches at these lower levels. Various red and white oaks are scattered throughout the periphery of the fields and the lower forests. Rhododendron thrives. Up on the mountainside the vegetation changes with altitude. There are more sugar maples; chestnut oak is more prevalent and at the top of the mountain at about 2700 feet mountain laurel has replaced the rhododendron. Pine trees are scattered about, but white pine seems to prefer the lower, more protected areas. Hemlock in much the same manner seems to do better in the more protected lower areas, but as of this writing is under great pressure from an insect invasion which is killing many of them.

Even the climate is different at the top of the mountain. Here winds howl unabated and deep snow accumulates while in the lower meadows only a cold rain falls.

Because of my isolation I could probably draw a line around my place and the State Forest that encompasses 25 square miles and I would be the only one living inside that line. Even on the other side of the river there are only a few people per square mile. My nearest full time neighbor is over a mile away to the west of the river. My mailbox is a mile away.

Chapter 2

PHILOSOPHY

For almost two decades while I was living in Cabin John, Maryland, a western suburb of Washington, D.C., I was employed by the Federal Government as a biologist. I worked with many animals, but for the most part I conducted experiments in basic science research. Concomitant with this period I was engaged in animal rehabilitation, working mostly on my own and with a few other rehabilitators. Everyone in the neighborhood knew I was the animal guy and would either tell me about injured or orphaned animals or bring them to me. The suburb was an older one set along a heavily wooded area along the Potomac River and the old C & O canal and towpath. In addition directly across the road from me lay another large uninhabited forested area with a year round creek. So in addition to the wildlife brought to me I would see much indigenous wildlife.

While I am not a veterinarian my experience doing operations on animals as a federal biologist gave me the confidence to perform many routine procedures. But, by the time an animal was brought to me with any serious injury its prospect for survival was so minimal that often euthanasia was the most humane treatment.

The rewards for trying to help wild animals are numerous. Just the concept of trying to help another living creature brings out all the altruistic qualities in a person. I am sure those that brought animals to me felt this sense of satisfaction. Obviously, another reward is the simple act of being able to interact with another creature in a positive way. This is especially true when raising babies.

I do believe that most of us regardless of sex have some maternal or parental instincts. Holding a baby skunk to your warm chest and watching it fall asleep or seeing its zeal for a bottle of formula makes all the efforts worthwhile.

And the satisfaction of bringing an animal back to health or to an age for release also has its rewards. Of course there are conflicting emotions when an animal is released. One is happy that that animal will now be able to be part of its natural environment, but one also now has to let go of that animal emotionally so that it can make its own way. Added to this is the fact that survival in the wild for any animal is much more tenuous than in captivity. It is estimated that an opossum in the wild survives no more than a year or two. I have had ones that could not be released live to be five years old.

Another tremendous reward occurs when you live in the middle of a release area. Most think that all animals raised by humans cannot either survive in the wild or become so accustomed to humans that they will become a nuisance. To some extent this is so, but there are many exceptions due to the uncanny ability of animals to discriminate and recognize us as individuals. In subsequent chapters I will describe some of the situations that happened with me.

Chapter 3

FAWNS

On Sunday May 29, 2005 two fellows, Shane Harvey and James Stoots, from Beckley, West Virginia brought me a new born fawn which they had helped to rescue from a lake near their home the day before. As they were riding their ATVs (all-terrain vehicles) near the lake they saw some boys trying to help this fawn out of the lake where it was in danger of drowning.

After pulling the fawn out of the water the fellows made sure its airway was clear and that it would survive. They then placed it in some nearby grass where its mother, if she was around, could find it. An hour or so later they returned to find the fawn where they left it. It still seemed weak from its ordeal.

Fearing the fawn would not survive they took it home and called the West Virginia Division of Natural Resources (DNR).

The woman who answered the phone told them that the DNR was not interested in either retrieving or helping the fawn. She further instructed them to simply put the fawn back in the "woods."

Realizing that this weakened animal would not survive such an ordeal they searched for options.

One of them had a computer which he used to look for anyone who could help this fawn. His efforts led him to call a friend of mine in the northern part the state. She gave them my name and number.

By talking to them I could tell that this little deer was in good hands for another day when they would bring me the fawn.

The arrangement was that when they got to Hillsboro about 6 miles from my place the next day they would call me so that I could drive across the river to meet them and pick up the fawn. We agreed on an estimated time of arrival. Their call came as anticipated, but they told me they were calling from a house just across the river from me. Unfortunately, that house belonged to Pete Treadway who disliked me intensely because I would not allow him to hunt on my place.

Needless to say Pete was elated to learn that these guys were bringing me a fawn. Pete knew that in West Virginia there was no formal mechanism for anyone to care for any orphaned or abandoned wildlife. And Pete himself had been charged in the past for the illegal possession of wildlife.

I have no doubt that Pete was salivating at the prospect of calling the DNR to report all that he heard and could see.

In reality, though, and in a more practical way almost all farmers in these eastern mountains of West Virginia have at one time or another cared for orphaned fawns.

I myself from the first year I moved to West Virginia had cared for at least one fawn each year till receiving this one.

As soon as the guys called me to tell me they were across the river with the fawn I got into my truck with Kip, my border collie and drove across the river.

Kip over the years had been my chief assistant at raising animals. He just seemed to know that his role was to protect and to watch out over any critter under our care. And he just seemed to know when a new arrival was at hand. In this light he just had to go everywhere with me.

So Kip jumped into the truck with me in anticipation of another fawn.

On the other side of the river, right in front of Pete Treadway's house, was the car with the guys and the fawn.

We exchanged greetings and they showed me the fawn. It was in great shape for almost drowning and for not having eaten in at least 24 hours.

I picked the fawn out of the back seat of their car and put it onto the front seat of my truck with Kip. With the door to the truck still open I took out my camera and took a picture.

I told the guys that I would send them a copy, thanked them and informed them that I wanted to provide some nourishment for this little fawn as soon as possible.

The guys left and I drove across the river and to home where I gave the fawn its first bottle.

Fawns are best raised on a milk replacement used for baby goats. This formula, which comes as a powder, is high in fat and has all the other nutrients and vitamins necessary. I normally used a ½ pint baby bottle where I slightly enlarged the nipple hole. This was just the right amount of food for each feeding so that the fawn was satisfied, but not too engorged. The powder is mixed initially with cold water and then I put the bottle into my microwave for just the right amount of time and at a power setting so that it heated to about 100-105 degrees F.

I kept the fawn in the bathtub of the bathroom so that it felt protected and safe. In nature fawns hide in the tall grass when their mothers are not around. In a couple of days the fawn learned to hop out of the bathtub and wander around the house. But it always returned to either the bathtub or the mat next to it when it wanted to relax or hide. Each morning the first thing I would do was to take the fawn outside to relieve itself. Failure to do this or to procrastinate insured that I would be cleaning up a mess from the floor. The feces from a newborn fawn can be very loose for the first week. Throughout each day I would take the fawn out not just for this purpose, but so that I could sit with it in the grass and have it become use to being outside and these new surroundings. From the moment I got the fawn I would whistle to it in a certain way every time I approached it or was with it. I wanted it to learn to recognize this call as though I was its real mother.

We humans are funny in the way we consider many kinds of animals and especially their babies endearing. Psychologically we easily embrace those babies who seem warm, cuddly, cute and vulnerable. Not only does a new born fawn fit this profile, but our culture fosters this image and feelings. As a human and as a biologist I understood the emotions, but also knew of the "trap." Yes, a fawn can be raised to be compatible with humans. Game farms do it all the time. But being compatible does not exactly mean "domesticated." And while my goal at raising wild animals has always been to have them grow up and become part of their wild heritage there is a fine balance I have to achieve so that any animal raised in this manner does not become so familiar with humans that it might become either a nuisance or dangerous to humans. That is why the location of my facility, Point of View Farm, was so important. Most, but not all small to mid-sized mammals have a home range that is fairly confined as long as food resources are available. A rabbit, a woodchuck, a skunk and even deer do not wander very far from where they are born or raised. Birds and reptiles are a different matter. Since I had thousands of acres of state forest bordering me and no human neighbors for over a mile across a river I could be pretty certain that any mammal I released back into the environment would quickly become part of the local ecology and not impinge on anyone else. At any given time there is a population of 30-50 deer that makes Point of View Farm their home base. And while hunting is allowed in the state forest access to it is not easy. One can enter from the east side five miles away, but to traverse from that point to the edge of my property would require very strenuous hiking through a series of steep mountainsides and valleys. To enter from the west requires one to cross the river. I do not allow passage via my driveway and when the river is high or covered with ice, crossing is almost impossible. Therefore, while it was always of some concern I did not think any of the fawns I raised and released would be walking up to a hunter to be shot. It was also my experience that fawns I raised in this manner easily and quickly integrated themselves into the indigenous herd.

I named my little new charge Aspen. And yes, for the first week I feared that the DNR might just try to make a visit. Technically, though, the DNR is not supposed to tamper with or kill an animal that is acting naturally in the environment. I say technically, because I know of several instances where they have done just this. But by taking Aspen outside, playing with her outside and even leaving her in high grass outside during the day she would not be visible to anyone wanting to search the cabin.

Since the DNR had refused to confiscate this fawn when called during the day by the guys who found it, I could not imagine that they would launch any kind of night time raid just to see if I had a fawn in the house. Besides I would have spotted them long before they reached the house and could have quickly taken Aspen outside again.

Raising fawns is in a way quite easy as long as you are attentive and present much of the time. They can be left alone for fairly long periods because once they are fed and satiated they will return to their place of shelter and sleep till called again for their next meal. Outside if I called, Aspen would follow me, but quickly became tired. After feeding it was easily hidden again. The darkness of my bathroom provided the ideal spot for the first week and allowed me to perform other chores for limited amounts of time.

As mentioned above despite this bond that can occur fawns and deer are wild animals. In the wild a fawn is never lifted off its legs. Humans caring for fawns will often try to pick them up. I did this all the time, but it is never something that a fawn found comfortable. Fawns in the wild are never lifted off the ground. From the moment I would get a fawn I would pick it up often so that it became acquainted with the process. Even a newborn fawn, though, is much stronger than it looks. With great quickness and strength it can suddenly thrash out with its long legs, wiggle its body and almost fly out of ones arms crashing down to the ground or floor risking injury. This strength and agility increases tremendously as the weeks go by.

The year before I got Aspen I was brought a fawn that a woman had tried to raise for a couple of weeks. She quickly discovered that the task was more than she could handle. The woman had tried to cuddle and carry the fawn only to find that it jumped out of her arms. Crashing to the floor the fawn had broken two of its legs. In addition she was not feeding it the correct formula and somehow it had become infested with fleas. The fawn had been named Blossom and by the time I got her the legs had begun to mend.

Since no one was officially authorized by the DNR to take care of wild animals it would have also been against the law for a veterinarian to help any such animal in need. Many vets might be willing to care for this fawn, but I at that time did not know of any who could help Blossom. I could not risk her being killed by the DNR by looking for such a veterinarian.

I was amazed at how quickly Blossom's legs healed once she was eating a proper diet, and it was easy to rid her of the fleas. Without difficulty she learned to come to my whistle and after a week or so quickly adapted to living outside. Living in the wild is in itself dangerous. After having her for about two months, I noticed something was definitely amiss. She was favoring her right leg and it was obviously broken. Perhaps she had stepped into a hole or "tripped" over something. At this point she was too big to carry and again trying to take her to a veterinarian was not an option. The break was not an open one and I could detect no gross separation of the bones. I crudely analyzed it as a hair line fracture of her radius bone. With agility she held it off the ground and moved about gingerly on three legs keeping her injured leg from bearing any weight. I made the decision to just keep as close an eye on her as possible hoping, like in the past that she might heal quickly without complications. My greatest fear was that she might fall prey to predators. Bears and coyotes easily took fawns and injured deer. Blossom would be an easy meal should she be spotted by such an animal.

Once during the spring when fawns were being born I was working on a project in front of my barn. Three hundred yards away was a creek, Oldham run, and a riparian wooded area. Suddenly, I heard a piercing scream and cry. Instantly, I knew that a bear had found a fawn. Kip, my dog, was by my side and he, too, knew what had happened. Together we ran over to the ford where I crossed the creek to see if we could locate the bear. I had a foot bridge over the creek and by standing on it I could see the bear a hundred feet downstream. The bear saw me and moved to one side of the creek. I moved in tandem only to see the bear dart back to the other side. Back and forth we did this little two step a couple of times till the bear decided that it wanted to not only come in my direction, but get by me. With a burst of speed it simply ran past me on the other side of the creek. Kip just stood and watched the activities.

Fortunately, I never had to hear the screams of Blossom in such a situation and again her leg healed quickly. She and Kip had played lots of games together and it is possible that Blossom learned to dodge away from predator attacks from her interactions with Kip. Over the years Blossom more than any other fawn I raised has maintained this familiar relationship with me and Kip. If she is nearby she will come to my whistle. I just love giving Blossom hugs, a scoop of grain and to just run my hands over her sleek coat.

But the potential dangers of maintaining contact with a deer raised from a fawn are very real. The first fawn I raised on Point of View Farm was a male I named Bucky, not because he would become a buck, but because everyone called my father Bucky. Bucky easily integrated himself into the wild population his first year, but like Blossom would come when he saw me or I whistled. He was truly amazing in that even when grown he would go for long hikes with me and Kip and even when I hiked with groups of friends. He even followed everyone back to the cabin to mingle. Inside the cabin he would nibble on food that had been left over on the dining room table. I even have a picture of him eating some pizza (see Chapter 23 picture). Visitors were amazed that a deer would do this. Throughout the winter and into his second year this relationship continued. By the summer of his second year he began to develop his first set of antlers. By early fall he had a modest 5 point rack that was beginning to lose its velvet.

The antlers on a deer grow and are nourished by a hefty blood supply provided by a layer of soft skin called velvet which is filled with blood vessels. Once a change in hormones signals that the underlying bone or antler has reached it maximum growth for the season, the velvet begins to die. It is thought that this "itches" and in order to relive this itch the buck rubs its antlers on trees or other surfaces to remove the velvet. At about this same time the testosterone that is flowing to its brain stimulates the buck into a mating mode. In a herd environment the mature bucks will engage in "fights" to establish which is the dominate male and have the privilege of mating with all the does.

The winner is determined by which buck, often with the largest rack or set of antlers, is strong enough to head butt and push the others around. In any herd even the lesser bucks will engage in and practice this procedure.

Bucky at this time of year was feeling his hormones. He still would go for hikes with me, but every once in a while when he was "feeling his oats" he would come up behind me and "challenge" me. While I was physically bigger than him, he was incredibly strong. If I wanted him to stop, I had to stop him. I found the only way to achieve this was to show him that I was indeed the stronger male. Often bucks when engaged in this fighting would rear up on their hind legs and whip at their opponent with their forelegs. I did not want this to happen because I could seriously be injured if his sharp hooves were to tear into me. I, therefore, engaged in such challenges using my mind as much as my brawn. My arms were long and more dexterous than his hooves or neck and antlers. By grabbing his antlers and using leverage I could twist and thrust him straight down toward the ground thus neutralizing his power and weapons. By holding him in this position for a while I could induce fatigue. When I finally let go he would be back to "normal" at least for a while. But all of this just points out that even a hand raised deer can be dangerous. Hunters have even run into this aggressive behavior.

Aspen followed the same pattern of development and assimilation into the deer herd on the property as all the others. Interestingly, by the time I went to trial she was out of my care and on her own. Unlike some of the others I raised she does not come back to me for handouts.

Chapter 4

THE INVESTIGATION

Two Conservation officers from the WV DNR operate in Pocahontas County. Both had been to my animal sanctuary in the past via an invitation. Both have seen the **NO TRESPASSING** signs just as you come out of the river onto the farm.

On one occasion I actually told the officer who was visiting that I took care of orphaned fawns. He said nothing.

Howard Shinaberry was one of the officers. He lived about 35 miles north of me. He came to my place several years before when I obtained a game farm permit to raise ring neck pheasants and bob white quail. I wanted to release them to see if they would establish breeding flocks. Howard and I had a pleasant visit. Howard and I even had a common bond.

A couple of years earlier I had adopted a "rescued" border collie which I had been told belonged to Howard's parents. Howard's father had died and his mother had been confined to an assisted living situation so she could no longer care for Kip, the dog. I asked Howard about this series of incidents and he confirmed that indeed I had his family dog. Howard thought the dog was about 15 years old. I could tell Kip was old, but did not suspect he was that old.

I called Shane Duffield, the other officer, once when I retrieved two bear dogs who had been wandering my property for several days. I wanted Officer Duffield to be responsible for returning the dogs to their owner.

Hunting bears with dogs that have been turned loose is a horrible spectacle. And here in West Virginia these so called "hunters" are allowed to "train" their dogs all year long. The "training" consists of releasing into the environment a pack of dogs that are generally hungry in order to have them chase game. Some or all of the dogs have radio collars that transmit back to a receiver and antenna carried by the "hunter." "Carried" is often a loose word because usually the hunter and his buddy simply ride around in a pickup truck.

The dogs run all over the countryside where they chase and kill almost anything. And of course they crisscross over everyone's property.

This "training" might go on for several days during which the dogs do not eat anything except the game they can kill.

In the spring and summer this is particularly tragic because fawns are killed; ground nesting birds including wild turkey hens are run off their nests and bears with new born cubs are sometimes chased for miles. These cubs are often separated from their mothers and killed. In such an instance if the cub cannot manage to climb a tree it is torn to shreds by the dogs. I have overheard these "hunters" brag about how their dogs killed bear cubs out of the hunting season.

At any time of year except during hunting season killing game is illegal, but it is even more egregious in the spring and summer because with warmer temperatures a full grown bear being run through the forest can easily expire from heat exhaustion.

Without any restrictions, the dogs at all hours of the day or night will, like a gang of screaming kids, come barking and howling right by anyone's home.

I can assure anyone that to be wakened in the middle of the night by 10 or more barking and howling hounds is disconcerting.

The guys who turn these dogs loose do not care one bit about what is happening to the environment, other animal life or the peace and quiet of anyone else. They may have released their dogs days earlier and for them it is just fun to drive around with their buddy in that truck. After all, who cares if the dogs have been running loose for several days? Who cares if the dogs have not been fed? In West Virginia it is all legal.

In their minds the hunters will eventually find the dogs because they have radio collars. Hey, it is part of the "fun."

I have had dogs wander onto the farm after having been released 20 miles away. I have seen them kill fawns. I have been unable to catch some that then wandered off into the wilderness in the middle of the winter at zero degrees. Isolated on my side of the river in such conditions the dogs had little chance of survival. Many such dogs die of cold, starvation, injuries or even drowning.

I have seen what happens when a pack of dogs corners an adult bear. The scene would make a fight in the Roman Coliseum between aggressive animals seem gentle. What happens in the forest between bears and dogs would make Michael Vick look like a choir boy.

And when I did carry dogs back across the river to give them to their owners, the hunters would often be very belligerent towards me.

I called one hunter after finding his injured dog. When he showed up, with distain he simply grabbed the dog by its front legs in one hand and its hind legs in the other, tossed it over his shoulder and walked away. The dog winced in pain.

These "hunters" dislike me immensely because I am very vocal about this cruelty to animals.

In the past I used to leave one of my vehicles on the "other" side of the river so that I had transportation if the river was too high to drive across. These bear dog guys, who had threatened me and promised "to get me" have busted up my truck by smashing the windows and slashing the tires.

Hence, my call to Officer Duffield, to have him return the dogs to their owners.

When he arrived he refused to drive through the river despite the fact that it was very low. I, therefore, had to cross to pick him up.

I had put the dog into one of my holding cages near some of my other animals. I showed him the dog and also told him about the fawns I had raised in the past and even remarked to him that I carried gingersnaps to give to the deer when they came out of the forest. He said nothing about this practice.

This silence on his part I later learned had legal implications.

Nevertheless, we loaded the dog into my truck, drove through the river to the waiting hunter. I gave the dog to Officer Duffield. He gave the dog to the hunter and that was the end of that.

Neither Officer Shinaberry nor Officer Duffield to the best of my knowledge came onto my property again until the end of May and the beginning of June, 2005 to illegally investigate the possibility that I had a fawn.

The day after I received the fawn I had to go to town to run some errands. I was only gone a few hours, but when I got back I noticed something very unusual about the house.

I have a precocious blue and gold Macaw parrot that will go outside by pushing open the storm door to the house if the regular door is ajar. I therefore make it a point to secure the doors by making sure they are tightly pulled shut.

When I arrive home from my errands I immediately noticed that both the inner and outer storm door to the house were partially open. My parrot, Ella, was still inside, but in my mind I was sure I had pulled the doors closed.

Because of the isolation of the farm and the difficulty anyone would have of crossing the river to "visit" I could not imagine anyone having come to the house in my absence. Besides nothing seemed out of place and the fawn was still in the bathroom where I had left her. Choosing to believe I had indeed left the doors open by accident I went about engaging in my other tasks for the day, including feeding the fawn.

However, in a telephone conversation with a neighbor who lived over a mile away, I learned that she had seen a WV DNR vehicle earlier that day. She could not identify the driver or where it may have been going.

On the other side of the Greenbrier River is a wonderful 80 mile hiking/biking trail that runs parallel to the river. At one time 30 or more years ago the "trail" was a railroad line that was mostly used to move logs from timbering out of the mountains. As the forests were finally stripped of most prime trees the railroad fell into decline and was taken out of service. In an ecofriendly move the State of West Virginia took control of the railroad right of way, removed the tracks, smoothed the bed and created this long hiking biking trail. Control of the trail was then assumed by the WVDNR.

Jody Spenser of the DNR has the responsibility of maintaining the trail. So it is not unusual for him or any of his workers to be on or near the trail and to have driven by my neighbor's home. I simply presumed that any vehicles owned by the DNR would have been those used for the trail.

The next day, Tuesday the first of June-2005 began in a routine fashion. I fed and cared for the fawn, took care of my other animals and worked on other chores. Later in the day a neighbor, Larry Dean, came over to help me at some of my more challenging tasks.

Over the past several months I had been having difficulty with all my muscles, as they were functioning improperly. My large leg muscles at times seemed to knot up or become weak. I had been using the drug Lipitor to help control a high cholesterol level so I decided to research its side effects. Immediately I discovered that muscle weakness could be experienced so despite my high cholesterol levels I went off the drug, cold turkey. And while I noticed some improvement, there were still some tasks which I could not do or could not do alone. Larry was a farmer living about 15 miles away who had helped me in the past and whom I could trust. Often he would call me to see if I needed any help.

On this particular afternoon while we were in front of the barn working on some of my machinery, I heard the sound of a vehicle in the distance and on my gravel road. My view from the barn extended only about a quarter of a mile to a point where the driveway crossed Oldham run. In a few moments the unmistakable sight of the green DNR vehicle appeared as it drove to the barn.

Well, now in my mind it all started to make sense. Stoots and Harvey had stopped at the home of Pete Treadway to call me about having the fawn. Pete hated me and now a DNR vehicle was driving on my property. As soon as I could see the driver I recognized him as Shane Duffield, the conservation officer who had been on the farm before when I had the bear dog. Of interest to me was the fact that when I had the bear dog, Officer Duffield refused to drive his DNR vehicle through the river to pick up the dog. Now here he was coming along my driveway in the same vehicle.

In the last 10 seconds it took for Shane to pull in front of me, stop his vehicle and get out I knew that he was not on a social trip.

I had a white tail deer fawn. The DNR was notorious for not caring about any individual animal. They had no provisions to care for such an animal nor did they want to show any such individual attention. The solution administered in such cases was a "final" solution. They simply shot such animals or as with Stoots and Harvey, instructed them to simply throw the animal back into the forest where it would die of starvation or be killed by predators.

The State of West Virginia also refused to allow any of the many private citizens who were capable of providing animal rehabilitation to help any such orphaned or injured wildlife. In this venue the State of West Virginia stands almost alone in its callous approach to these situations. As a matter of fact the WV DNR specifically has lobbied in the past against any legislation which would allow for animal rehabilitators like me to exist in West Virginia. The bottom line is that any orphaned or injured wildlife found by any person is immediately sentenced to death if the WV DNR knows about it.

I liked Shane Duffield, but he did not even bother to telephone me to ask me any questions about the possibility of my having a fawn and he did not call me to ask if he could enter the property. So, there he was getting out of his official vehicle, wearing his official uniform and carrying a gun.

I, now a surrogate mother to this fawn for the past couple of days, was not about to relinquish this animal in such a situation. By the time Shane exited the vehicle I was already in my defensive, protective mode with the hair on the back of my neck standing out straight and with my adrenalin flowing.

Realizing that I had to take control of this situation I shifted to an offensive mode. I do believe I said hello to him, but before he could possibly respond I ask him to produce a search warrant which would allow him to even enter the property. In the process I reminded him that he had just driven through several No Trespassing signs and that he could not simply come onto the property willy nilly.

He responded by telling me that Officer Howard Shinaberry had been to the property the day before and had "looked around".

"Ahhhhah," I thought, "now I knew why my door was open and why my neighbor saw a DNR vehicle."

Being even more aggressive I again pressed Shane for any warrant and inquired as to any warrant Officer Shinaberry may have had to search my property.

It was obvious that my posture and position took him by surprise. In hindsight I believe he thought that he could legally trespass on private property to check out a telephone complaint by Pete Treadway. And in hindsight I think that the possibility exists that nothing would have happened had I told him about the fawn or even shown it to him. But, I could not risk the life of the fawn to simply be accommodating to a man in uniform.

Not only did he have no warrant, but I am sure he did not even know what I was talking about. I even informed him that absolutely nothing he did, saw or discussed with me could be used in any law enforcement manner. And I told him that I was really disappointed that he would attempt to violate my constitutional rights. I even told him not to even ask me about any fawns because I would not answer nor would I allow him to inspect any of the out buildings or the house. My goal was to establish my rights and the rules by which he could proceed.

The conversation continued, at times in a somewhat heated manner. In order to try to diffuse the animosity that was building I asked him if he would like to see some of the raptors I had under my care.

From a previous visit Shane Duffield was aware that I had permits from the United States Fish and Wildlife Service to care for migratory birds. These permits are independent of any rules or regulations in the State of West Virginia. As a matter of fact West Virginia Code specifically recognizes these permits.

My large flight cages for housing these birds are about 3-400 yards from the front of the barn where we were engaged.

Together we walked through the field to the cages and there I showed him each hawk or vulture and explained its reason for being under my care. This seemed to relieve some of the tension. In these more rational moments Shane told me that Howard Shinaberry had been at the main office in Elkins on that Monday morning when the call came in from Pete Treadway complaining about my having a fawn. Howard Shinaberry was then dispatched to check out the complaint by Mike Pizzino, the Captain of the DNR for our section of the state. This Howard did when I was not home. Exactly how or why the case was transferred to Officer Duffield was never made clear.

We then returned to his vehicle and he left.

I have to admit that for the rest of the day I was filled with emotion about the way I handled this situation. On one hand I was scared because never would I have thought that I would stand up so forcefully to a law enforcement officer, but on the other hand I was proud of myself for having stood up the way I did. Nevertheless, it was quite possible that either Shinaberry or Duffield would obtain a valid search warrant and return.

Via the United States Constitution a search warrant is valid only if it is accompanied by an affidavit from someone asserting that the objects being sought in some way violate the law and that the object(s) are likely in the possession of a suspect or on the site to be searched. In addition the search warrant has to be specific as to what objects are being sought. A search warrant cannot simply say that a property is going to be searched for anything suspicious.

So to some extent for a couple of days I became a little paranoid that either or both of these officers would be back to search for the fawn. To counter this I simply fed the fawn in the morning and then put it outside in tall grass near the house.

New born fawns are programmed to remain still and under cover usually in high grass while their mothers leave them to feed. While they are perfectly capable of walking around, a newborn fawn is so vulnerable to predation that their chief defensive mechanisms at this early age are a lack of scent, ability to be perfectly still and to use their spots to blend in with the environment. Bears, eagles, coyotes, bobcats and domestic dogs are the chief killers of newborn fawns.

Since the fawn, that I had named Aspen, was so young I knew that after I fed it I could place it outside in a protected area and it would not move. Also very quickly fawns learn the voice of their mother. In my experience when I condition fawns to a whistle they will come to me out of hiding to be fed. Pavlov, the Russian physiologist in the 1890s discovered that when he whistled to his dogs at feeding time they would associate his whistle with feeding whether or not he was going to feed them. I also knew that the policy of the DNR was not to take fawns out of the wild just so they could kill them. It was much easier on the officers if they simply left a fawn alone. Nevertheless, I also knew that I could not trust any of the officers because killing animals was part of their routine and that protecting their jobs would always be more important than saving an animal.

These latter points proved true when Howard Shinaberry later shot and killed a grown fawn in a small community called Cass. The fawn had been raised by one of the citizens of Cass and in a way was the town pet. The community was outraged. Without cause Shinaberry not only shot and killed this deer, but then lied to the person who raised it about what he did.

A similar incident occurred in Lewisburg, a town about 40 miles south of me. There a dog and a fawn were playing on someone's field when a DNR officer illegally trespassed on the property and killed the fawn while he uttered vulgarities to keep the property owners at bay. In each case the Director of the DNR, Frank Jezioro, cleared the officers of any "wrong doing."

By hiding my fawn each day in the wild I calculated that if these officers showed up again they would not find the deer.

With everything calm and quiet the next day I called Mike Pizzino, the captain in charge and the person who dispatched Shinaberry and Duffield. In an inquisitive manner I simply asked him what he and the DNR planned to do about the situation. He told me that the decision about how to handle this would be in the hands of Officer Duffield.

Well, to me that was encouraging, so I called Shane. It had been 24 hours since our altercation. To me he seemed like he could be a rational person who might be able to separate his uniform from an act to save a baby fawn. We talked for quite a while. In the end he said that the decision about what to do would be up to Captain Pizzino. Instantly I knew that that one or both of them were liars. .

I followed these telephone calls up with one to Howard Shinaberry two days later. Again I talked with Howard for quite a long time, but it was obvious that he had no clue as to what he could do legally and what he could not. Howard had worn the uniform for several decades, but it was obvious that when it came to law enforcement he understood little beyond that he could hand out "permits" to his friends who wanted to kill game out of season by claiming crop damage. Howard did know enough to arrest hunters who did not have licenses, but as far as being a student of his legal and constitutional responsibilities he was deficient and highly challenged.

At this point I could have just allowed the system to do its thing and involve me if that was to be my fate. But, I am of the mindset that the more I know the better off I am. Besides I felt all along that I had not done anything wrong. Just because West Virginia did not have a formal animal rehabilitation program did not mean that individuals, like me, could not help wildlife legally.

When I came to West Virginia I came with my non-profit charitable organization called Point of View Farm, Inc. Point of View Farm had been granted 501 (C) (3) status with the U.S. IRS and labeled as an animal sanctuary. In addition I had applied for and obtained a business license for West Virginia. My application stated that my business activity was to aid abandoned and needy wildlife. The Secretary of State, Joe Manchin Jr. III, stated that my application conformed to law, approved the business license and issued to me a Certificate of Authority to carry out my business activities. Mr. Manchin later became the governor of the State of West Virginia. These two documents, in my mind, satisfied the exact criteria as stated in the West Virginia laws.

The next week with these documents in hand I went to the court house to chat with Walt Weiford, the county prosecutor.

The court house is located in Marlinton, WV, the Pocahontas County seat. Only about 1000 people live in Marlinton which sits on the banks of the Greenbrier River. With heavy rains the river floods into Marlinton and at times people have drowned. Some have called for the entire town to move. Others want the U. S. Corps of Engineers to spend 100 million dollars on a levee system.

The courthouse sits at a spot furthest from the river and has not been damaged by the river. Built in 1876 the building is of historical value and does possess an old time charm. One can access the building through several entrances, but unlike its counter parts around the country this courthouse does not have any guards frisking employees or visitors, nor does one have to enter through any metal detectors. I dare say that if one were to come into the courthouse with a shotgun the only question would be "how many squirrels did you get?"

In addition to Mr. Weiford there was an assistant prosecutor, Tony Tatano. Two magistrates have offices in the court house. While one magistrate hears cases in the lower part of the county for a week the other will staff an office in Durban about 40 miles north. Each alternates their time. The sheriff's office is also located in the court house as are the other more normal court house functions. Since the main office for the two circuit court judges is in Lewisburg in Greenbrier County just to the south of Pocahontas County only a single Circuit Court office is maintained in the Pocahontas County courthouse along with a courtroom on the second floor. Halfway up the stairs to the circuit court chambers sits a metal detector, which I have never seen operational.

The two magistrate judge positions, the two Circuit Court judges, the sheriff and the head prosecutor are elected individuals. The assistant prosecutor is hired by the prosecutor. Case volume is usually pretty low with about 5-10 cases weekly in each court.

Across the street from the court house a small building houses family court and its judge, another elected position.

So on Wednesday the 8th of June, 2005 I met with Walt Weiford and explained what had happened. To my surprise he was very accommodating.

Mr. Weiford had grown up in Pocahontas County and had been elected prosecutor for many terms.

He told me that he was glad that I was in the county helping animals and that the county needed someone like me. "Just go home, take care of the fawn and don't worry about it," he said.

So there I was with the blessing of the county prosecutor. He had the power to choose which cases he would prosecute and which he would not. And while at this point no charges or anything had been filed I felt I was "home free." So even if the DNR were to try to charge me I was at this point protected by Mr. Weiford.

I have to admit the 20 mile trip back home felt pretty good. Now I did not have to worry about this fawn or any other. And that evening after I called Aspen from the grass with my whistle, fed her and put her back in the house for the night I slept peacefully.

By the next day, however, something began to gnaw at me. As much as I appreciated Mr. Weiford's words and gesture, all he was doing was saying that under his kind paternalism I would be protected. But what if he died, changed his mind, was voted out of office or had to give up his position? Who would protect me then? Besides, I thought that all my actions were within the law anyway. Over the next few days I allowed these thoughts to mull around in my mind and by the next Monday I knew I had to return to Walt's office.

There I told him that I fully appreciated what he had told me, but that not only did I believe that all my actions were lawful I wanted to be charged. This startled him and he inquired as to why I would want to be charged.

I told him that by being charged I hoped to demonstrate that all my actions were legal. I said, "I knew nothing about criminal law, but I needed a good academic exercise." I told him, I knew nothing about how everyone in the justice system really did things and I wanted to find out, that I did not like the way the DNR killed animals and I wanted to publicize their crude acts of killing.

Well, my first lesson in the law was to learn that the prosecutor does not file charges. Charges are brought by someone in law enforcement either on the basis of their own investigation or by allegations made by a citizen to law enforcement. The prosecutor simply drops the charges for lack of evidence or prosecutes them. Very rarely are charges dropped when they are brought directly by law enforcement. So Walt Weiford could not charge me directly. I would just have to wait and see what the DNR was going to do since they were official law enforcement officers.

Over the next few weeks nothing seemed to be happening so each time I went to town I stopped in the courthouse. If Walt was on a break I would quiz him about how the law worked and what might happen if I were charged. I really was about as green at this as one could be.

To his credit Walt Weiford would spend a few minutes with me each time I showed up to explain another facet of the law and what my possible response might be. Since I had not been charged with anything at this point his helping me was in no way a conflict of interest. Besides I think he enjoyed my calling him my "law professor."

His office was on the second floor just opposite an outside door to the building where there was a small balcony to a set of steps leading to the ground a floor below. Often I would find him on a cigarette break on this balcony which I adopted as "my office."

While even today he does not agree that he helped me that much, I found our sessions not only instructive, but very helpful psychologically in preparation for all that later unfolded. Besides just for me to understand some of the terminology and jargon made me feel that I was at least learning this new legal language.

Chapter 5

While shivering in my shoes
I strike a careless pose
And whistle a happy tune
And no one ever knows
I'm afraid

THE CHARGE

My mailbox is not at the house like most other persons. To retrieve my mail I have to drive three quarters of a mile along my gravel road to the river, ease into the river and slowly, drive 450 feet through the Greenbrier River to make very sure I do not flood the engine, exit the river and drive another third of a mile along my access road. There I cross the Greenbrier River hiking biking trail and stop at my mailbox on Beard Road the first asphalt surface.

When I went across the river to pick up the mail on the 8th of August, I was surprised to find a letter from the Magistrate's office of Pocahontas County. Inside was a form summoning me to appear before the magistrate for arraignment. The envelope also contained a copy of the Compliant against me as described by Officer Shane Duffield of the West Virginia Division of Natural Resources.

I was being charged with a misdemeanor criminal violation of WV Code 20-2-4, "the illegal possession of wildlife." Maximum penalty was a fine of $300 and 100 days in jail. My Case Number was 05-M-381.

The statement at the top of the page said that I had committed this "crime" on the 2nd of May, 2005. Given that I did not even get the fawn till 29th of May, weeks after the fawn was even born, I knew this was going to be an interesting case. The document was signed by Kathy Beverage, Magistrate on the 3rd of August, 2005.

The Complaint, itself, described the transfer of the fawn from Stoots and Harvey to me in front of Pete Treadway's house, but again stated that this "crime" took place on or about "05-2-05."

The form also stated that I was given till the 16th of August, 2005 to appear before Magistrate Beverage for my arraignment and plea.

Well, now it was formal. I was being charged as a criminal and would have to really find out how justice works in Pocahontas County, West Virginia and the United States of America first hand. It would be OJT, On the Job Training. No turning back now. I was in the system.

Early the next day, the 9th, I went to the courthouse and sought out Magistrate Beverage. She filled out and read to me a two page "Initial Rights Statement" which included the charge. I initialed the line on the first page where I gave up my right to have an attorney represent me and dated and signed the page at the bottom.

On the second page she set "bail" at a $100 PR, which stands for personal recognizance. Well, that seemed strange since personal recognizance meant you did not have to post bail.

She also asked me if I wanted a jury trial, to which I stated "yes." And then she and I dated and signed the second page.

At this point I have to admit and demonstrate how green I was. I thought that by telling her I wanted a jury trial that I would automatically get one. But I had failed to read the entire document and there in plain English it said that I had to also inform the court in writing within 20 days if I wanted a jury trial. This would later become a fascinating part of the proceedings.

Two other pages accompanied my arraignment. They both were part of what was called the "Criminal Bail Agreement: Cash or Recognizance." As a part of it I signed and agreed to pay the $100 bail. I guess they felt that I was a risk of flight and might just run away forever. Several parts of the agreement were quite puzzling. For this simple misdemeanor charge I had to notify the court every time I wanted to leave the state of West Virginia. I had to agree not to violate any state or federal laws and to agree not to have any contact with any "victims" in this matter. I am not sure if they considered the fawn to be a victim or not.

It should also be noted again that at no time did anyone ask me if I had the fawn, nor did anyone ever ask me to relinquish any fawn, nor did anyone in law enforcement try to legally search and seize any potential contraband.

In my mind it was the equivalent to being charged with the possession of drugs, and then having the police say "we know you have the drugs, but you can keep them."

No trial date was set at this time or on any of the documents

Chapter 6

The result of this deception
Is very strange to tell
For when I fool the people
I fear I fool myself as well

TREADWAY'S IRE

At the same time I was in limbo, between obtaining the fawn and being charged, the WV DNR began to initiate an investigation of Jonathan Harvey and James Stoots, the two fellows who saved the fawns life and brought it to me.

Pete Treadway not only had called a DNR telephone hot line about my having the fawn, but had copied down the license plate number of the car the fellows used to bring the fawn to me.

Treadway had been convicted on other occasions of illegally killing wildlife out of season. The fellows who had previously owned my property did not live on the farm and were not around in the fall. Each year Treadway took it upon himself to trespass on the property and hunt whenever he wanted. When I became the owner I prevented him from coming across the river to hunt. He resented me for this.

Now, he saw his opportunity when I got this fawn.

Initially he was told by the prosecutor that I was not going to be charged, but with sheer persistence he called any and every authority he could to make sure he could get "even" with me and Harvey and Stoots.

Ironically, I gave James Stoots a call the day another officer of the DNR had contacted him. The officer, Chris Lester, wanted to meet with Mr. Stoots.

I decided to call Lester and explain the situation to him. Rather than being friendly and understanding Officer Lester was crude and indignant to me. In his mind these guys had broken the law and he was going to do his best to bring about justice. For a half an hour he and I engaged in a tense conversation.

I found out that he was new to the force and very young. I tried to explain to him that the guys were just following the orders of the DNR by bringing the fawn to me so that I could release it. I told him over and over that I had the fawn. But with all of this he rambled on about how if they went to work in North Carolina he was going to go after them if they did not meet with him. Finally after he calmed down and I thought he understood the situation such that he would not be filing charges against Stoots and Harvey I told him that I would call the Stoots and Harvey and tell them to meet with him.

This I did much to my chagrin because Officer Lester really only wanted to make a "bust." He did not care about the circumstances. So at the end of July both Harvey and Stoots received summonses to appear in court for the illegal possession of wildlife. At a later date I obtained copies of these citations and was aghast at how illiterate a person was Officer Christopher Lester.

All the details of their "trials" elude me, but suffice it to say that both were as confused as I was at that time and were unable to defend themselves. Both were convicted and had to pay substantial fines. I did not even know that they were charged and convicted until they appeared much later as witnesses for the State at my trials.

Pete Treadway was not finished. I found out that in order to make sure I was charged he made many calls to both Walt Weiford and the law offices of the DNR in Charleston. Single handed he made sure I would go to court. He was obsessed with trying to have me convicted.

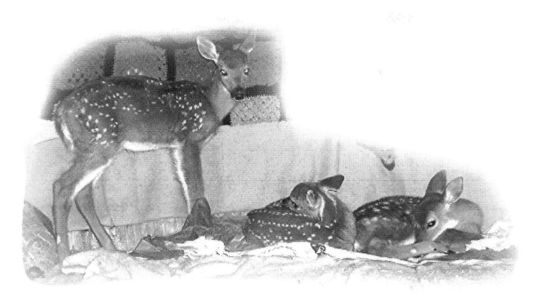

Chapter 7

I whistle a happy tune
And every single time
The happiness in the tune
Convinces me that I'm not afraid

STATUTES

WV Code §20-2-4. Possession of wildlife.

Except for wildlife, lawfully taken, killed, or obtained, no person shall have in his or her possession any wildlife, or parts thereof, during closed seasons. It is unlawful to possess any wildlife, or parts thereof, which have been illegally taken, killed or obtained. Any wildlife illegally taken, killed or possessed shall be forfeited to the state and shall be counted toward the daily, seasonal, bag, creel and possession limit of the person in possession of, or responsible for, the illegal taking or killing of any wildlife. Wildlife lawfully taken outside of this state shall be subject to the same laws and rules as that taken within this state. Migratory wild birds shall be possessed only in accordance with the "Migratory Bird Treaty Act" and regulations thereunder.

The restrictions in this section do not apply to the director or duly authorized agents, who may, in any manner, take or maintain in captivity, at any time, any wildlife for the purpose of carrying out the provisions of this chapter.

Wildlife, except protected birds, spotted fawn, and bear cubs, killed or mortally wounded as a result of being accidentally or inadvertently struck by a motor vehicle may be lawfully possessed: Provided, That the possessor of such wildlife shall provide notice of the claim within twelve hours to a relevant law-enforcement agency, and obtain a nonhunting game tag within twenty-four hours of possession. The director shall propose administrative policy which shall address the means, methods and administrative procedures for implementing the provisions of this section.

Above is the statute under which I was charged. Now that I was an accused criminal and one who was going to defend himself I knew I had better learn the law and fast. So the first thing I did was study the above statute in depth. Fortunately, I figured the first five words, **"Except for wildlife lawfully taken"** were the key. My mind turned first to the events which brought the fawn to me.

James Stoots and Jonathon Harvey had contacted the DNR and were told that the DNR would not come to pick up the fawn and that they were to release the fawn back into the wild. My intention was to do just that; release the deer back into the wild after I cared for it till it was able to fend for itself. So all I was doing was obeying the instructions of the DNR. I did not take the fawn from the wild and I had no intention of keeping the fawn, injuring or destroying it.

Second I knew that when I set up my nonprofit charity, Point of View Farm, Inc., I applied for and got a business license from the State of West Virginia. The application I filled out said that my business activity was to "care for abandoned and orphaned wildlife." I was issued a business license and a Certificate of Authority to carry out my business activities by the Secretary of State, Joe Manchin, Jr. III.

Half way through the wording of Statute 20-2-4 is the statement: **"The restrictions in this section do not apply to the director or duly authorized agents."** Well, in my mind I had a Certificate of Authority making me an agent of the State to help wildlife.

I further knew that one did not have to be an "agent" of the DNR because of the following line in Statute 20-2-4: **Migratory wild birds shall be possessed only in accordance with the "Migratory Bird Treaty Act" and regulations thereunder."** This sentence specifically relinquishes all authority for the possession of migratory birds to the Federal Government. And I had permits to possess migratory birds from the U.S. Fish and Wildlife Service.

Further research into the law brought forth the following statute on "Cruelty to Animals:

WV Code §61-8-19. Cruelty to animals; penalties; exclusions.

(a) If any person cruelly mistreats, abandons or withholds proper sustenance, including food, water, shelter or medical treatment, necessary to sustain normal health and fitness or to end suffering or abandons any animal to die, or intentionally, knowingly or recklessly leaves an animal unattended and confined in a motor vehicle when physical injury to or death of the animal is likely to result, or rides an animal when it is physically unfit, or baits or harasses any animal for the purpose of making it perform for a person's amusement, or cruelly chains any animal or uses, trains or possesses any domesticated animal for the purpose of seizing, detaining or maltreating any other domesticated animal, he or she is guilty of a misdemeanor and, upon conviction thereof, shall be fined not less than three hundred nor more than two thousand dollars or confined in jail not more than six months, or both.

(b) If any person intentionally tortures, or mutilates or maliciously kills an animal, or causes, procures or authorizes any other person to torture, mutilate or maliciously kill an animal, he or she is guilty of a felony and, upon conviction thereof, shall be confined in a correctional facility not less than one nor more than five years and be fined not less than one thousand dollars nor more than five thousand dollars. For the purposes of this subsection, "torture" means an action taken for the primary purpose of inflicting pain.

(c) Any person, other than a licensed veterinarian or a person acting under the direction or with the approval of a licensed veterinarian, who knowingly and willfully administers or causes to be administered to any animal participating in any contest any controlled substance or any other drug for the purpose of altering or otherwise affecting said animal's performance is guilty of a misdemeanor and, upon conviction thereof, shall be fined not less than five hundred nor more than two thousand dollars.

(d) Any person convicted of a violation of this section shall forfeit his or her interest in any animal and all interest in the animal shall vest in the humane society or county pound of the county in which the conviction was rendered and the

person shall, in addition to any fine imposed, be liable for any costs incurred or to be incurred by the humane society or county pound as a result.

(e) For the purpose of this section, the term "controlled substance" has the same meaning ascribed to it by subsection (d), section one hundred one, article one, chapter sixty-a of this code.

(f) The provisions of this section do not apply to lawful acts of hunting, fishing, trapping or animal training or farm livestock, poultry, gaming fowl or wildlife kept in private or licensed game farms if kept and maintained according to usual and accepted standards of livestock, poultry, gaming fowl or wildlife or game farm production and management, nor to humane use of animals or activities regulated under and in conformity with the provisions of 7 U.S.C. §2131, et seq., and the regulations promulgated thereunder, as both statutes and regulations are in effect on the effective date of this section.

(g) Notwithstanding the provisions of subsection (a) of this section, any person convicted of a second or subsequent violation of said subsection is guilty of a misdemeanor and shall be confined in jail for a period of not less than ninety days nor more than one year, fined not less than five hundred dollars nor more than three thousand dollars, or both. The incarceration set forth in this subsection shall be mandatory unless the provisions of subsection (h) of this section are complied with.

(h)(1) Notwithstanding any provision of this code to the contrary, no person who has been convicted of a violation of the provisions of subsection (a) or (b) of this section may be granted probation until the defendant has undergone a complete psychiatric or psychological evaluation and the court has reviewed the evaluation. Unless the defendant is determined by the court to be indigent, he or she shall be responsible for the cost of said evaluation.

(2) For any person convicted of a violation of subsection (a) or (b) of this section, the court may, in addition to the penalties provided in this section, impose a requirement that he or she complete a program of anger management intervention for perpetrators of animal cruelty. Unless the defendant is determined by the court to be indigent, he or she shall be responsible for the cost of the program.

(i) In addition to any other penalty which can be imposed for a violation of this section, a court shall prohibit any person so convicted from possessing, owning or residing with any animal or type of animal for a period of five years following entry of a misdemeanor conviction and fifteen years following entry of a felony convic-

tion. A violation under this subsection is a misdemeanor punishable by a fine not exceeding two thousand dollars and forfeiture of the animal.

As one can see from the opening line (a) to have simply thrown the fawn out into the wild would have itself been a crime more severe than simple possession. And the statute says "any animal" not just a domestic animal. Besides no one, not even the WV DNR can instruct a citizen to break the law.

West Virginia law is broken down into chapters. Each chapter covers a specific area of the law, e.g. labor, human services, taxes. Chapter 20 is the Natural Resources chapter. It was therefore imperative that I read all the statutes in Chapter 20.

And low and behold there staring me in the face was another statute which I hoped would be helpful. Statute 20-2C- 1 and 1 (h) as listed below, seemed very useful.

WV Code §20-2C-1. Governor's authority to execute.
ARTICLE I. FINDINGS AND DECLARATION OF POLICY AND PURPOSE.
(h) "License" means any license, permit or other public document which conveys to the person to whom it was issued the privilege of pursuing, possessing or taking any wildlife regulated by statute, rule, regulation or ordinance of a participating state.

Here again was confirmation that the Governor had "powers" over wildlife, not just the DNR. This statute confirmed, to me, my authority to possess wildlife not only through my business license, but by the ruling and public documents of the U.S. IRS granting charitable status to Point of View Farm, Inc. for the prevention of cruelty to animals and to house and aid injured and orphaned wildlife.

Throughout this process of my legal education someone would throw out a concept to me not only to enrich my knowledge, but to also provide a legal basis for my defense.

Prior to receiving a date for any court hearing I began to meet with the Assistant Prosecutor, Tony Tatano, who would be handling the case for the State of West Virginia. In a crazy way Tony and I established an interesting personal relationship in addition to our legal one.

Tony was about 40 years old, married and had a young, cute as a button, daughter, Rebecca. As soon as I met him I could tell he was compromised medically. He was a heavy man, but much of his weight was fluid. He was bald and his face and head was flush and red and showed lesions from some sort of bodily reaction. My immediate thoughts were of some sort of immunological situation.

I immediately inquired of his condition. Several months earlier he had been in an automobile accident and needed a back operation. The surgeon used some cadaver parts as replacements for his own.

Often bones from cadavers are harvested for use in healthy people who need operations. Such parts can contain blood and HLA (tissue) antigens different than the recipients, but this danger is usually neutralized with special treatments of the tissue.

Unfortunately, Tony was suffering from what is termed a graft verses host disease. This is where the cadaver bone graft or tissue implant actually attacks the patient as it grows. These situations are very serious and are usually treated with steroids which curtail the immune system. This treatment has its own side effects which include fluid retention and an increased risk of infections.

Tony did not look well.

Despite my being a total tyro to the law I tried to hold my own during our meetings while at the same time learning as much as I could. One of the first concepts discussed was the aspect of "**criminal intent**". Ironically this same term would later be used by one of the justices of the West Virginia Supreme Court of Appeals in my case.

Tony tried to explain the use of the term and how, in many situations, it cannot be a factor. For instance if you walk into a store with a gun and try to steal money you have criminal intent even if you do not get any money. But if your vehicle suddenly slides on some "black ice" on the road and injures someone else in another vehicle the collision is usually determined to be an accident without criminal intent and no charges would be filed. But if you are driving along and do not pay attention to your speed you can be charged with driving too fast even though you had no "intent" to commit a crime. The presumption being that you have a responsibility to watch your speed. With me Tony argued that as long as in his view I had illegally possessed wildlife intent was not a factor. In his opinion I should have been aware that my actions were illegal. And like a motorist who speeds he declared me guilty.

As a further insult he sat back in his chair and pontificated with a wry smile as to what other charges he might file against me.

I should note at this point that the Supreme Court in West Virginia, in the case of State v. Boyd defined the role of the prosecutor as follows:

The prosecuting attorney occupies a quasi-judicial position in the trial of a criminal case. In keeping with this position, he is required to avoid the role of a partisan eager to convict, and must deal fairly with the accused as well as the other participants in the trial. It is the prosecutor's duty to set a tone of fairness and pursue the State's case, in so doing he must not abandon the quasi-judicial role with which he is cloaked under the law.

And in another case: No. 25844 - State of West Virginia v. Walter Lee Swafford, II, Justice Starcher of the WV Supreme Court similarly opined.

By this time I was up to my eyeballs in what I was facing, but to show an air of false security I just intimated that the more charges he brought the better. Rocking forward in his chair, putting his elbows on his desk, tipping his head down a bit he exclaimed that of course he could ask the judge to reduce the fine if I agreed to plead guilty. I thanked him and said we would talk again.

One of my goals was at this time being met. I was learning how the legal system worked and of the powers of the prosecutors and the State.

At home I contemplated my options over and over. To me my tough stance seemed noble, but was it prudent? After all I still had the fawn. No one even seemed to care about her, except me. I could easily just cop a plea and walk away with a small $25-$50 fine. And Walt Weiford would help to keep me relatively safe from further charges.

I paced around the farm trying to put into perspective the chances of little, ole me, without any legal training, up against the unlimited resources of an entire state.

I called a friend, Bob Higdon, who was a trial lawyer. Not only was he not interested, but he thought the entire matter to be useless. He advised me to plead guilty and pay the fine. And with little fanfare he indicated that he wished not to be bothered with any further questions. At least he could have given me encouragement to stand my ground no matter what, I thought.

I wanted to do this, to learn the law, to see how the whole court system worked, to expose the DNR and to win my case. But as I paced the farm my feeling gyrated from despair to determination. At times I became actually scared at what was happening. At other times I would sing out songs as loud as I could. I sang three songs more than any others. In the Broadway musical, the King and I, Anna the teacher sings "I whistle a happy tune" to describe what she does when she feels afraid. The lyrics are:

I Whistle a Happy Tune

Whenever I feel afraid
I hold my head erect
And whistle a happy tune
So no one will suspect
I'm afraid.

While shivering in my shoes
I strike a careless pose
And whistle a happy tune
And no one ever knows
I'm afraid.

The result of this deception
Is very strange to tell
For when I fool the people
I fear I fool myself as well!

I whistle a happy tune
And ev'ry single time
The happiness in the tune
Convinces me that I'm not afraid.

Make believe you're brave
And the trick will take you far.
You may be as brave
As you make believe you are

You may be as brave
As you make believe you are

While shivering in my shoes
I strike a careless pose
And whistle a happy tune

And no one ever knows,
I'm afraid.

The result of this deception
Is very strange to tell
For when I fool the people
I fear I fool myself as well!

I whistle a happy tune
And ev'ry single time
The happiness in the tune
Convinces me that I'm not afraid.

Make believe you're brave
And the trick will take you far.
You may be as brave
As you make believe you are....

The other songs I loved to sing were "The Impossible Dream" and "Man of La Mancha" from the musical, "Man of La Mancha." The lyrics are:

The Impossible Dream

To dream the impossible dream
To fight the unbeatable foe
To bear with unbearable sorrow
To run where the brave dare not go

To right the unrightable wrong
To love pure and chaste from afar
To try when your arms are too weary
To reach the unreachable star

This is my quest
To follow that star

No matter how hopeless
No matter how far
To fight for the right
Without question or pause
To be willing to march into Hell
For a heavenly cause

And I know if I'll only be true
To this glorious quest
That my heart will lie peaceful and calm
When I'm laid to my rest

And the world will be better for this
That one man, scorned and covered with scars
Still strove with his last ounce of courage
To reach the unreachable star

Man of La Mancha

I am I, Don Quixote,
the Lord of La Mancha
Destroyer of Evil am I
I will march to the sound of the trumpets of glory
Forever to conquer or die

Hear me heathens and wizards and serpents of sin
All your dastardly doings are past
For a holy endeavor is now to begin
  And virtue shall triumph at last

I am I, Don Quixote, the Lord of La Mancha
My destiny calls and I go
And the wild winds of fortune will carry me onward
Oh whither so ever they blow

I sang these songs hundreds of times and they surely did give me motivation to continue. Each time I walked around one of the ponds on the property I would bellow out these songs to help me muster the strength to believe that my quest was noble and correct and worthy of pursuit.

I used another motivational tool to keep me focused. My middle name is David and I would tell Tony and Walt that like the biblical David I always carried rocks of just the correct size for my sling so that I could slay any Goliath who ventured into range.

When I was quite young, television was just becoming a normal household appliance. A huge portion of those early shows were "cowboy" movies. The story line in almost every case was one where a rancher was being preyed upon by some nefarious character, often the sheriff or the judge, who wanted to steal his land. But the hero, Roy Rogers or Gene Autry, would come along to instill encouragement in the rancher, outwit the villain and then marry the rancher's daughter. Never did the villain prevail in any of these stories. I watched hundreds of movies with this same theme and to me, a mere lad of 5-10, the message was clear. If you fought for truth, justice and the American way you would prevail.

Even now all of us are inspired from time to time by movies about people who stand against tyranny and win or who overcome long odds to succeed.

Here in West Virginia a heart-warming story known to most is about the "Rocket Boys." In 1957 when the Russians launched Sputnik the world was captivated. In a small coal mining town in West Virginia Homer Hickham was the teenage son of a coal mining foreman. Sons were expected to follow in their father's footsteps. But Homer became smitten with rockets and was determined to have a better life for himself. He and his friends learned about and began building rockets, which led to winning a county science fair project and finally winning a national contest. College scholarships followed and indeed Homer went on to be a rocket engineer. One of our astronauts even carried into space one of Homer's gadgets.

Homer wrote books about his experiences and a 1950s movie, "October Sky" is about his experiences.

Even in the animal kingdom such motivational stories are known. A horse named Seabiscuit born in 1933 was an ungainly colt that was small, knock-kneed and had a propensity for only sleeping and eating. His first trainer was unsuccessful as Seabiscuit lost all of his first 17 races. For the next couple of years, Seabiscuit did win a few races, but had at best a mediocre career. By 1936 he had been sold.

The new owner having seen something special in Seabiscuit trained him differently and by 1937 the horse won 15 of 17 races. Then at the height of the depression Seabiscuit showed the stuff of champions. He won all but one of his races and in the "race of the century," a match race between him and War Admiral, the horse of the year in 1937, Seabiscuit won easily. In that year the talk of America was about Seabiscuit and he took "Horse of the Year" honors in 1938.

Of course now as an adult I know that the "good guy" does not always win and that one places himself at risk if he is willing to separate himself from the flock and face the "wolves" alone.

I knew that I could never mentally survive if I was not willing to challenge the State from my own position of braggadocio. Even if my lack of knowledge made this stance somewhat of a bluff I needed to do it to help challenge myself.

Another tactic I used for my own mental stimulation was to write members of the WV DNR in an attempt to demonstrate my lack of fear of them. To this end I sent letters to Mike Pizzino, the captain of my DNR district, and the one who ordered me to be charged. I also sent a long letter to Frank Jezioro, the Director of the WV DNR.

I was not only determined to reject Tony Tatano's "offer" for me to plea bargain my case with a proclamation of guilt, but to make a defiant statement. I therefore, told him that not only would I not plead guilty, but that he could not pay me $10,000 to do so and that I was going to fulfill my goal of whipping him and the State of West Virginia.

Ironically, one thing I feared was that Tony at the direction of Walt Weiford might actually drop the case against me. After all Walt did tell me that he liked the fact that I was here in Pocahontas County and that I was needed. But I later learned from Walt himself that he got calls from Lieutenant Larry Case, a high official in the DNR in Charleston, WV. Case took a personal interest and wanted to make sure I was not only prosecuted, but convicted. Now in my idealistic mind that was an illegal tampering.

From a more practical standpoint I had to study the law, court procedures and methods of defense. To this end the internet became my indispensable conduit into the legal system. There was no way I could have learned as much as I did without the access to laws, statutes and court cases and opinions through the Internet and its link to the World Wide Web. Defending oneself in the court system involved more than just knowing some laws. I also had to learn the format for drafting motions, appeals, responses and briefs as well as the mechanisms of filing these papers. At the court-house I picked up some of this information by looking at archived cases. And by ask-ing the clerks for help, I quickly learned the best mechanism for not just filing these papers, but for making sure that all parties received their copies.

Since I had no in court experience of representing myself I knew that I would be at a huge disadvantage to any manipulations and tricks Tony would try to throw at me. There is a whole set of court procedures and terminology that I not only had to learn, but understand how to use. I considered going to the courthouse to observe real trials, but later discovered that I could do this more efficiently by simply watching Court TV on television. The show had cameras in courtrooms around the country showing how real life situations develop. By watching these trials I was able to see and learn not only much of the procedures that I would need, but I could see how some lawyers were better than others. The shows also had prominent lawyers and judges analyze, during the breaks, what was happening in the courtrooms.

Here I learned so much, not only about how the courtroom operates, but about tactics and strategies, about methodologies to sway the court or the jury and about the value of positive presentations. Granted the cases on Court TV were much more involved and of a more serious criminal nature than my case, but that only allowed me to see how a defense team had to really fight to keep their clients out of jail.

From watching these cases on TV it became apparent that the two most hack-neyed terms in court are the words "objection" and "hearsay." Basically hearsay is a term that describes any statement made by a witness that is attributed to what some-one else said. So for instance a witness cannot tell the court that he heard that Uncle Bob said he saw the incident. But, this entire concept becomes murky quickly. An officer can tell the court that Uncle Bob told him that he saw the incident and that is why there was an investigation. One can see that the two statements are very similar and that there is not much distinction. In the first case the witness is just making an off the cuff remark about what he heard Uncle Bob say. In the second case the witness, an officer, was told directly by Uncle Bob that he saw the incident. Usually, depending on the case, if Uncle Bob really saw the incident he would also be a witness. In my case I could ask the guys who brought me the fawn what the DNR told them when they called about finding the fawn, but I could not ask them if they had heard some-one say that the policy of the DNR was such and such.

The other most used term in court is an objection, which includes an objection of hearsay, or for lack of foundation, or lack of relevance. Objections run the full range of ideas. Objections are voiced about the certainty of evidence, to the standing of a witness, to the qualifications of a potential "expert" witness, to the "badgering of a witness," to a certain question posed to a witness, etc. Almost immediately following an objection the other side will chime in with why they feel the question or statement is valid. The judge will then either sustain (confirm) the objection or overrule it and allow for the testimony or evidence.

Objections are very important especially for the defense because they often lay the foundation for an appeal should the judge overrule the objection. It is because of this that while an objection may not be warranted it is best to lodge one anyway and have it overruled to make sure that a judge's ruling can be challenged on appeal. In jury trials objections are often pivotal on appeal when a judge either allows or does not allow evidence or testimony to be considered by the jury. Usually judges understand all of this and consider it part of the maneuvering that takes place in a courtroom. Sometimes, though, in lower courts a magistrate will take exception to this courtroom jockeying and think that the tactics are directed against him or her. Obviously this can be "dangerous" because the magistrate might start ruling against one side or the other because of this prejudice. I learned firsthand that magistrates despite their oaths of office will form personal and prejudicial opinions that influence their decisions.

Chapter 8

Make believe you're brave
And the trick will take you far.
You may be as brave
As you make believe you are

THE LEARNING CURVE

Trial was set for the fall of 2005, and I knew that my lack of knowledge and experience needed to be changed quickly. To this end I studied as much as I could about my rights, procedures and the words of the law. But I also knew that one of my glaring weaknesses was that I had no court experience. How would I handle myself in front of a Magistrate, while I represented myself? I needed courtroom experience.

Somehow I discovered that I could have the court convene if I filed motions. I also discovered that the magistrate who would handle my trial was not Kathy Beverage who signed the complaint against me, but Doshia Webb, the other magistrate in the county. Kathy was to have double knee surgery and would be indisposed for many months.

Interestingly, Doshia had a few years earlier been a DNR officer and in that capacity had actually given me animals to care for. Surely, I thought having done this she could not convict me of a crime of illegal possession. And when I saw her in the hall of the courthouse she even remarked how she thought the case was stupid. I, also, knew that she left the DNR because she had filed a sexual harassment case against the DNR and won. I even voted for her when she ran in the previous election to become a magistrate. Of course she would be fair and reasonable, or so I thought.

So my campaign to get court time experience and for justice began in earnest.

From the old court cases I perused in the courthouse I learned that copies of all such filings also had to be given to the State (the prosecutor) and that each document had to have a "certificate of service" stating under oath that indeed a copy was given to the opposing party.

When I submitted motions to have the case dismissed Doshia would conduct a hearing on the matter so that I could present my arguments and have Tony object to them... The irony was that while I argued intently for each motion I actually wanted the case to continue.

Because the complaint against me alleged that I had gotten this fawn four weeks before it was even born I submitted a motion to have the case dismissed on this point. How could I commit a crime of illegally possessing an animal that was not even born? In the law the state has to show *actus reus* or that an illegal act has been committed.

I also motioned for dismissal saying that none of my actions comprised any criminal intent. How could helping out an orphaned fawn be construed as my having a mind of criminal intent? This concept is also within the legal term of *mens rea* and indeed it was the duty of the prosecutor to demonstrate *scienter*, which implies that I had some mental intent to commit a crime. Besides, I argued to the court, how could the very magistrate before me have given me animals to take care of and then think that I was guilty of a crime by taking care of an animal?

In talking with many of my neighbors and farmers throughout the county I found out that many had at one time or another raised orphan fawns. And in many of these cases the DNR knew about the activity. Thus, I learned about the term *Selective Prosecution* where a fairly common, possibly illegal activity is not prosecuted except against one person whom the DNR might not like. I, therefore, argued for a motion of dismissal based on *Selective Prosecution*. This concept also later flowed off of the lips of one of the Justices of the WV Supreme Court.

Inherent in this same theme of *Selective Prosecution* is the concept of the *Doctrine of desuetude*. The reasoning here is that if a law has not been applied for ages even though the activity is common then a dismissal of the charges is warranted because the law has either never been used, is antiquated, or only rarely applied in the past. An example of this might be a statute that says it is against the law to tie your horse to a porch post on Main Street. Then a hundred years after horses were last used for transportation someone in a parade ties his horse to a porch post and is arrested. The defendant could argue for a dismissal based on the *Doctrine of desuetude*.

Using the computer in the courthouse, I looked for any case where someone had been charged because they took care of a fawn and I found none. On this basis I filed another motion for dismissal based on the *Doctrine of desuetude*.

In the law if an officer knows a certain activity is occurring and does not tell the person doing the activity to stop, but later charges the person in regards to that activity a defense of an *estopple by Silence* can be launched. This simply means that the action or charge against you has to be stopped because of the silence of the officer. For instance if every day you were to cross a street with an officer at the same spot, but he did not tell you that you were jaywalking and that this was a crime you could say that the officer had a *duty* to tell you of your "crime" the first time. And that you are innocent of any wrong doing by an *estopple by Silence* if he later tries to charge you. Granted this is a tricky legal position because one could say that ignorance of the law is no defense. But isn't it the duty of the officer to either charge you the first time or at least not be silent on the matter?

In my case I had told Officer Duffield that I had raised fawns and even showed him cookies I carried for them on one of his past visits. I, therefore, motioned for dismissal on this basis.

I don't remember who it was, but someone who learned of my being charged told me to look up the term "Statutes in *pari materia*." This I did and found it very apropos to my situation. This term simply means that if two statutes address the same material, they can and should be considered together when adjudicating a case. So in my situation I was being charged with the illegal possession of wildlife, WV Code 20-2-4, but a cruelty to animal statute 61-8-19 stated that it is illegal to abandon any animal. In my mind it should be illegal for one to be placed in a catch 22 situation whereby no matter what you do you could be breaking the law. To me these two statutes were in

Pari materia and should be reviewed together in order to have the charge against me dismissed. And on this basis I filed a motion to have the charge dropped.

I also motioned for dismissal saying that not only did I not remove the fawn from the wild, but that when Stoots and Harvey contacted the DNR they were told to put it back in the wild. Since the DNR cannot instruct a citizen to violate the law of abandoning the fawn they sought me out so that I could put the fawn back in the environment while still taking care of it. The fawn would not be abandoned.

Since, I felt that I was authorized to care for wildlife because of my business license I motioned for dismissal on this basis. I had submitted an application to the Secretary of State, Joe Manchin, Jr. which stated that my business activity would be to aid abandoned and needy wildlife. Mr. Manchin said that the application "conformed to law" and I was issued a business license. Mr. Manchin signed a Certificate of Authority allowing me to conduct my business. In every way, I felt, this alone conformed to the provisions of WV Code 20-2-4.

But, I argued, further, that my public document from the IRS granting Point of View Farm, Inc. charitable status clearly stated that the activities of the organization were to not only prevent cruelty to animals, but to "establish a wildlife rehabilitation center to house and rehabilitate wounded, maltreated and/or endangered and local species." This conformed to not only WV Code 20-2-4, but to WV Code 20-2C-1(h) which says that one can possess wildlife if the activity is part of a public document.

Article I Section 10 of the U.S. Constitution says: **No state shall enter into any treaty, alliance, or confederation; grant letters of marquee and reprisal; coin money; emit bills of credit; make anything but gold and silver coin a tender in payment of debts; pass any bill of attainder, ex post facto law,** *or law impairing the obligation of contracts,* **or grant any title of nobility.**

It was obvious to me that when the United States IRS granted me charitable status it was contingent on my following certain conditions. In essence this was a contract between Point of View Farm, Inc. and the United States Government. As president of Point of View Farm, Inc., I was obligated to carry out the conditions and activities of the contract. Consistent with this I reasoned that the State of West Virginia could not enforce any law that would impair the obligation of this contract. With this knowledge I filled another motion for dismissal based on this Article of the U.S. Constitution. In a similar fashion I argued that my business license with the State of West Virginia was a contract in that I had to conduct my business as I described in my application to aid abandoned and needy wildlife. As with all the above motions, this was also denied.

By filing all of these motions I forced the magistrate court to hear them providing myself with much needed court room experience. At each court hearing concerning my motions I presented court cases and rulings to support my motion. At first I stumbled around a little when facing Tony, the prosecutor, and Doshia, the Magistrate. After all I was a real, raw rookie.

But I quickly got the hang of things and felt that not only were my arguments solid, but that Doshia might just follow through with her idea that this was all stupid and dismiss the case. Well, not only did she not dismiss the case, but it quickly became obvious that I was indeed going to find out exactly how "justice" was meted out in the courthouse in Pocahontas County. I was getting the court experience I wanted, but about all Tony had to do was say he objected and Doshia would throw out my motions.

A friend of mine who was an attorney once told me that he faced a judge who routinely denied all his motions without even reading them. So he filed a motion to have all illegal motions denied. He did this "tongue in cheek" to confirm that the judge did not read them and indeed the judge denied his motion which meant that the court would accept illegal motions. My friend finally got his case dismissed because of this judge's stupidity.

I learned that I would also be denied a jury trial based on the fact that I did not notify the court in writing that I wanted one. Well, I also found out that the magistrate at arraignment is also supposed to tell the accused that he must submit the request in writing. This was not done so I filed a motion noting this faux pas. This motion, too, was denied.

Since Plan "A," filing motions in regards to the law had failed, I then implemented plan "B," attacking the integrity of the court. My first act was to file a motion asking Doshia to recuse herself because she had been a DNR officer and in that capacity had given me animals. Doshia refused to remove herself from the case. So I filed a request with the circuit court judge to have her disqualified. He, too, refused to remove her.

Since it has been shown many times that an officer wearing his uniform in court commands more respect and credibility from a jury than a "civilian," I submitted a motion requesting that all the DNR officers wear civilian clothes rather than appear in their uniforms when they testified. This, too, was rejected.

Another motion I filed which actually was accepted was to have only the witness who was testifying to be allowed into the courtroom during the trial. I did not want witnesses from the DNR all hearing the testimony of the others so that they could coordinate their testimonies.

In West Virginia the DNR has neither a mechanism nor a desire to care for and save any wildlife compromised by injury or by being an orphan. They simply kill any such animal. For me to have relinquished my fawn, Aspen, to the DNR would have meant that I was a conspirator to this destruction. In law one cannot engage in *moral turpitude* which is to violate standards of decency towards other life. To participate in an unwarranted killing of this fawn I reasoned would be to violate the law in this regard. I, therefore, submitted another motion for dismissal arguing that I had a legal obligation to conduct myself in a moral and ethical manner. As with my other motions it, too, was denied.

With all these motions I not only began to hone my court skills, but more and more became stimulated academically to think in terms of being able to present a thorough legal defense. My guess is that no one in the history of Magistrate Court in Pocahontas County has filed as many motions as I did. At each motion hearing it became obvious that by simply exercising my rights I became a thorn in the side of the judge as well as the prosecutor. After all in both their minds I was guilty no matter what and that no defense, no matter how valid was going to sway Doshia, the magistrate, to make the correct legal decision. But this was one of my objectives, to learn how the system and those in the system really worked.

Another important fact that I learned, but I cannot remember from where, was that while one is always trying to win the case that is before them it is very important to bring up every point possible via motion, testimony or objection should an appeal be necessary. Technically, one cannot appeal a lower court conviction on grounds not brought forth in that lower court.

It also dawned on me even at these early stages that a "real" lawyer could never do all what I was doing no matter how much he/she might be paid. After all, even a defense lawyer is an "officer" of the court and would never be caught "badgering" the court. Because I was not a lawyer I could approach my case without any ties to the legal fraternity that formalized the relationships between the court, judges, prosecutors and defense attorneys into a bland, vanilla interaction regulated by lots of pomp and circumstance, but often little substance.

Chapter 9

While shivering in my shoes
I strike a careless pose
And whistle a happy tune
And no one ever knows,
I'm afraid.

DISCOVERY

Very quickly I felt that my ability to handle the pressures of being before a judge and dealing with a hostile prosecutor improved. Doshia's rulings against me and her blatant display of prejudice actually built my confidence. I now knew that my efforts would be more to establish my positions than to actually win a judgment.

My court time was also enhanced, however, by another facet of the system. As an accused criminal I had the right to request via "discovery" any information, documents or evidence that the State planned on using or that I thought would help me with my defense. To this end I submitted to Tony and Walt a list of items I wanted.

Being green and naïve I put together what I thought was a thorough list of items I needed for my defense. This request for discovery is listed below:

All qualifications, courses taken and grades achieved in law and wildlife biology by Mike Pizzino and all performance records. All records of his contact and communications with Officers Shane Duffield and Howard Shinaberry from 29 May, 2005 through 5 September 2005

All records, tape recordings, actions, E mails, telephone calls, logs, conversations, reports, memos, documents and anything else received or produced by the DNR in regards to this case, to especially include anything emanating from or about Capt. Mike Pizzino, Capt. Dan Farley, Lieutenant Lawrence Case, Major Murphy, Col. Fields, Dir. Frank Jezioro, Officers Shane Duffield, Howard Shinaberry and Lester Christopher and William Lilly.

All reports, logs, diaries, notes, tape recordings, dispositions and E mails of Officer Shane Duffield for the last two years dealing with wildlife

All reports, logs, diaries, notes tape recordings, dispositions and E mails of Officer Howard Shinaberry for the last 5 years dealing with wildlife

All reports, notes, dispositions, logs, and E mails filed with the Captain Mike Pizzino from all wildlife biologists operating in his district for the past two years

Any training manuals, books, schedules used by the DNR for the training of Conservation Officers, to include any refresher courses.

A list of all courses taken by Conservation Officers dealing with West Virginia Law and United States Constitutional Law

A list of all refresher courses in Law taken by Conservation Officers Shane Duffield and Howard Shinaberry

A list of all courses taken by Conservation Officers about the proper methods of dealing with wildlife

A list of all qualifications and skills Conservation Officers must obtain to deal with Wildlife

A list of all the qualifications and skills DNR wildlife biologists must obtain to deal with wildlife.

A copy of the reports, records, logs, and the disposition of all calls about wildlife handled by any member of the DNR in West Virginia during 2004 and 2005

A copy of all performance reports for the past five years for both Officer Shane Duffield and Officer Howard Shinaberry

A copy of all complaints filed against Officer Shane Duffield and Howard Shinaberry

All reports, memos, logs, records and E mails from Lt. Lawrence Case, DNR Charleston, WV. In regards to his contact with DNR officer Christopher Lester, Captain Dan Farley, Shane Duffield, Mike Pizzino and Walt Weiford about this case. Also all phone logs for June and July from Lt. Case's office.

All notes, reports, memos, E mails and logs of Conservation Officer Christopher Lester of the DNR in regards to his investigation of anyone related to this case.

Copies of all DNR publications about wildlife to include all pamphlets, newspaper and magazine articles and all authored papers in any scientific or laymen journals by DNR wildlife biologists.

Copies of all studies done about wildlife in West Virginia by anyone in the DNR or supported by any grants or contracts from the DNR, or the state of West Virginia from the years 1990-2005.

Copies of all citations issued to Earnest "Pete" Treadway or any member of his family.

Copies of all complaints from Earnest "Pete" Treadway or any member of his family at HC 64 Box 136 Hillsboro, WV 24946 and Fayetteville, WV.

A list to include dates of all contacts, telephone calls, E mails and visits made between the Pocahontas County Prosecutor's office and members of the DNR in regards to this case.

And yes I was green and naïve because I thought I would be entitled to all of this information. After all it is easy to see how I could use all of the documents. But by this time Walt was no longer my "law professor." We were now antagonists. And as a way of demonstrating the power of the state he and Tony refused to give me almost all of the information requested.

One of the most amazing aspects of this quest of mine to learn the law was that as the State and the Magistrate became more recalcitrant to grant what I considered were my rights I actually learned more than if they had simply been cooperative. The more they tried to stonewall me the more I tried to figure out how to counter them. So since I was not having much success with my "Requests for Discovery," I found another method and another term to learn.

All along I had planned to use both Officer Howard Shinnaberry who searched my place without my being present and Officer Shane Duffield who I confronted in front of my barn for his illegal search, as witnesses. Shane would have to appear in court since he was the officer who filed the complaint. Every defendant in a criminal case has the right to face and examine his accuser. My accuser was Shane Duffield so I did not have to subpoena him for the trial. But I would have to subpoena Howard Shinnaberry.

When doing some basic research on subpoenas I quickly found the term "subpoena *duces tecum*." And to me this was a wonderful find. It literally required the recipient of the subpoena to bring with him/her under penalty of punishment any information, evidence or documents requested. Ahhhhh, what a find! Now I had another tool to get the information I wanted; stick it to the State and put them a bit on the defensive themselves. I, therefore, filed a subpoena *duces tecum* to Captain Mike Pizzino, requesting the information that Walt Weiford and Tony Tatano would not give me.

To my total amazement this simple act gave me a power I never could have envisioned. Of course I had no idea as to how various agencies of the West Virginia government operated from a legal standpoint. I was now to learn.

As it turned out each state agency had assigned to it a lawyer from the state Attorney General's office. It is the job of this lawyer to represent the agency in any legal or court matters. And as I found out the first job of that lawyer is to "protect" any member of that agency from cooperating with any subpoena or court order.

Well, color me super naïve again. If asked I surely would have said that all employees of the State are employees of the citizens of the State. The idea that a lawyer hired by the citizens of the state could work for an agency of the state to thwart legal inquires in a criminal case was mind boggling to me. But this is exactly what happened.

In October of 2005 I along with the court and the prosecutor's office received a motion from one Kelley M. Goes, Assistant Attorney General to quash my subpoena *duces tecum*. Ms. Goes it turns out was the lawyer assigned to the West Virginia Division of Natural Resources and whose job it was to do her best to "protect" all her charges in the DNR, to thwart justice and to stonewall the judicial process.

By this time, though, I knew that the more I could get anyone from the State to put their thoughts and positions into writing the more mistakes they would make and the more fodder I would have for attacking them. Indeed Kelley Goes fell right into this trap. She must have spent hours drafting her six page response to my subpoenas.

I have to admit at first I felt somewhat intimidated by her lengthy reply. After all I thought she was a lawyer from the Attorney General's office so she should know what she was doing. But I read her motion again; and then I read it again and then a few more times. With each reading I realized that it was not only replete with errors, but that I truly had jerked some chains in the DNR office in Charleston and the Attorney Generals' office. It was clear that Kelley Goes wanted the court to just accept her motion and quash on the spot my subpoenas. I was not going to let this happen without a fight.

Implementing a strategy to force Ms. Goes' into more activity I filed a motion to compel the DNR to honor my subpoena *duces tecum* and at the very least to honor my right to have a hearing on the matter. Given that the State of West Virginia was being represented by the prosecutor's office of Pocahontas County I filed another motion arguing that Kelley Goes had no standing in my case and her motion to quash my request should not even be considered.

To my amazement Magistrate Webb had to fulfill this request by scheduling a hearing on the matter brought up by Ms. Goes. By now I surely was learning about the power and versatility of a motion.

Kelly Goes in her motion to quash my subpoena had declared that a crime had been committed and that I was the guilty person. This I could not believe. To my virgin ears she as a lawyer for the State could not make that statement since I had not been found guilty of anything at this point. She also opined as to how I should handle my own case. I, therefore, filed a motion for my case to be dismissed because Ms. Goes had prejudiced the court with her illegal assertions that I had committed a crime and because of her interference as to how I should handle my defense. Her statements proclaiming my guilt in her motion to quash, I argued deprived me of due process as provided by the 14th Amendment of the U.S. Constitution. This clause reads as follows:

Section. 1. All persons born or naturalized in the United States and subject to the jurisdiction thereof, are citizens of the United States and of the State wherein they reside. No State shall make or enforce any law which shall abridge the privileges or immunities of citizens of the United States; nor shall any State deprive any person of life, liberty, or property, without due process of law; nor deny to any person within its jurisdiction the equal protection of the laws.

By asking for the case to be dismissed with prejudice I wanted the court to affirm that the State had prejudiced its case against me and could not re file it. Had it been dismissed without prejudice it would have simply been an indication that the state had made an error and could re file the case if it corrected the error. An example of this was when the original complaint filed by Officer Duffield stated that I had committed the crime of possession the fawn on the 2nd of May four weeks before it was even born. Had Doshia acted properly she would have dismissed the case with this motion without prejudice to give the State an option to re file with this date corrected. As it turns out Officer Duffield tried to correct this error of his complaint via a motion of his own. Doshia accepted his motion.

Little did I realize that by requesting a hearing on the matter of Ms. Goes' motion to quash my subpoena I would force her to drive 3 hours from Charleston, WV, the state capital. I know that I use the word amazing over and over, but for me this was truly amazing. Because I had helped a fawn I was now forcing a lawyer attached to the WV DNR from the Attorney Generals' office to come all the way to Pocahontas County so she could argue that I should not be able to have information necessary to defend myself. At this stage of my "legal" career I obviously did not know how my case would end, but I sure was getting every single mile out of my rights.

The Magistrate court room is a tiny rectangle of a room in the basement of the Courthouse. It measures 14 feet by 20 feet. There is a desk for the magistrate, a chair next to the desk for the testifying witness, a set of tables and chairs for the prosecutor and the defendant and his lawyer, a few chairs near the door for any spectators, a chair for the bailiff and a set of chairs against the wall for a jury. There are no windows in the room and no ventilation. Nor is there any way to heat or cool the room except by the movement of air from the hallway. When occupied by just a few people and with the door closed, the room quickly becomes warm, humid and uncomfortable. Protocol places the prosecutor for the State to the left of the magistrate and the defendant to the right as the magistrate faces us. The prosecutor is closest to the jury and can literally touch the closest juror. Likewise any witness is right next to the jurors' chairs and could reach out to touch the closest juror. I was lucky in that at least two of my friends attended almost every hearing as spectators.

From my standpoint the hearing in regards Kelley's motion to quash my requests was psychologically won by me the moment Ms. Goes entered the courtroom. Of course Tony was there, too, so I was now up against two of the State's lawyers. With nothing again to lose I knew that the more I could keep them fighting me the more I would learn. After all I had already laid down a whole list of reasons to appeal should I lose at trial.

I introduced myself to Kelley and bantered with her for a while. As I stated above the more I felt I could engage my opposition the more I just might learn. It is amazing how much I discovered just from little chit chat. In short order I found out that she lived just outside Charleston, WV, was married to a man who was a prosecutor and that she had two children. But most importantly I discovered she had driven to Marlinton with Colonel Fields the top law enforcement officer in the DNR. I was sure that her having company for the long ride was helpful, but I wondered why such an officer would volunteer to just go for a "ride" in the country. Didn't he have more important things to do while on the job?

The answer to this question would come later and was most revealing. It seemed he and Doshia Webb, the Magistrate Judge, were "friends." And it seemed that after my hearing she and Colonel Fields went to lunch together.

I had told Walt Weiford that one of my objectives was to see how everyone operated in the Courthouse. At the very least for Colonel Fields of the DNR to have met with and then have had lunch with Doshia Webb, was inappropriate, a potential conflict of interest and a breach of court etiquette. At the most it was criminal if indeed Colonel Fields discussed my case or indicated to Doshia that I should be convicted.

So the plot thickened as did my challenges. I was up against all the big guns of the State of West Virginia and all because I had helped a fawn and refused to back down or go away.

The hearing got underway in a cordial manner. Kelley went through her reasons for wanting the subpoena quashed, but I argued vociferously that the information I sought was critical to my defense. From time to time Tony Tatano, the assistant prosecutor chimed in. I had asked for a great many things as a part of the theory that the more you ask for the more you might get.

One by one my requests were denied, but in the end Doshia did rule that my desires for the weekly logs of Officer Shinaberry and Officer Duffield along with the information about the original telephone call from Pete Treadway should be turned over to me.

I did receive from Walt and Tony some disturbing papers. They were copies of the charges brought against both Mr. Stoops and Mr. Harvey and the judge's findings of guilt.

I had spoken with Officer Christopher Lester about Stoots and Harvey in good faith and had thought that he would leave them alone. But now I found out that this "blankety blank" had filed charges against them and that they had been convicted. I was so mad that I added this to my bag of motivations to "get" the DNR and expose them for the laggards they were.

After the hearing, Kelley did send me the appropriate weekly reports filed by Officer Duffield and Officer Shinnaberry. Given what I now saw as gross incompetence by the WV DNR, I was not surprised that these reports were devoid of any useful information. Almost every day was blank indicating that they did not work or did not know how to write.

Each DNR officer because he lives and works long distances from the headquarters of each DNR district is basically on his own unless instructed by his captain to do something. Therefore each day an officer does what he wants and the only way of even knowing that he might have worked is by the weekly report he fills out. It is all predicated on his honesty. What a system. Neither Duffield nor Shinnaberry mentioned anything about me, coming to my farm or about the allegation that I had a fawn.

Finally, I received some of the other documents I requested. These included the complaints against Stoots and Harvey, the report from Officer Lester Christian and a copy of the original call put into the DNR by Pete Treadway.

These documents from Discovery did yield useful information. I learned that Shane Duffield, 6 days after I got the fawn, had gone to both Tony and Walt to file the charge against me. They both informed Officer Duffield that they would not prosecute for such a trivial matter. Duffield then informed Pete Treadway of this decision. I later discovered that Pete went ballistic and not only kept complaining, but that he contacted the DNR hierarchy in Charleston in an effort to force the matter. And even more disturbing I found out that Walt Weiford, the prosecutor for Pocahontas County was contacted by Larry Case from this DNR office insisting that I be prosecuted. This I believe is an illegal tampering by a government official. He should have been charged and convicted of a felony.

Because all my motions required hearings, the original trial date was continued or postponed.

Chapter 10

The result of this deception
Is very strange to tell
For when I fool the people
I fear I fool myself as well!

MY SUPPORTING GURU

In a way I could not have represented myself so well without John Leyzorek, a friend of mine. John is not a lawyer, but he is smart; book smart and street smart. I talked with him often.

John came to these mountains about 25-30 years ago from New Jersey. There he had a small piece of property, worked as an engineer, but wanted to find a place where he could have greater personal freedom in order to live a more basic lifestyle. In Pocahontas County he bought 600 acres high in the mountains and lived a simple life without electricity or running water. His only concessions to the outside world were

61

his vehicle and a telephone line. John had a wife and six beautiful kids. John's contribution to me was through his avocation for legal matters and his continual quest for knowledge. In addition he had an innate command for how the laws of the land were supposed to protect us.

I had met John a few years earlier and our mutual desire for knowledge almost dictated that we would become friends.

I don't know how many times I called John to get his opinion on something I was writing to the courts or to read him a response from the State. It was amazing how he could quickly grasp a situation, boil it down to some basic rights and simply reassure me.

How simple some of his responses were, yet they helped me lay out the foundation necessary for me to actually represent myself.

Of course telling all of these people who spoke for the State that they did not know the law or that they were violating my Constitutional rights, was like stabbing them in their collective sense of power. And the more I did this the more I could tell just from their body language that I was stepping on powerful toes and digging a deeper and deeper hole from which I had to somehow climb.

John always assured me that as long as my facts were correct I should not wavier from my quest.

From a stylistic standpoint John and I differed dramatically. John had had some experiences dealing with the enforcement of statutes when he was on a few committees and citizen's boards that had to make legal decisions. His approach was to always try to be as much like a lawyer as possible so as not to confuse the issue.

From my standpoint I knew I was not a lawyer and did not want my fate to be judged totally by that standard. I was an individual with individual and human emotions about what was happening. It was impossible for me to have presented my case in such a dry, formal, matter of fact manner and then hope for the best. At every hearing and with all my writings I had to insert emotion and passion along with the facts. At all the court hearings the "normal" and "acceptable" decorum was for everyone to be seated and to present their arguments from that position. This I could not do so I stood for all of my presentations. Yes, sometimes I sat when Tony Tatano or Kelley Goes were talking, but not always. I just felt much more comfortable standing to show the court that I was ready and able to say what needed to be said. Besides by standing I felt that I not only had more confidence at what I wanted to say, but that I had control over everything and everyone in the courtroom.

At one hearing Tony was seated a couple of chairs to my right and trying to make a point when he seemed to stumble a little on his words as if he suddenly became a little tongue tied. I immediately mentioned to him that he should relax and then I leaned over to him and gave him a hug and told him everything would be OK. Everyone laughed.

My approach to every court appearance was to not only act appropriately, to present every fact I knew, to fight passionately for my cause, but to also allow everyone to know that the entire process was also instructive, educational and enjoyable.

Because John attended all of the hearings he was able to give me his first hand assessment of what had happened. This was always helpful.

At one of my trials I asserted that Tony had lied to the court when he said I had not given him certain documents. John later signed an affidavit affirming what really happened.

Because John's lifestyle was one of being outdoors much of the time, either doing projects around his home or dealing with his animals, his normal attire in court was reflective of his true character as a mountain man. He wore work clothes, a ragged hat and Wellington, knee high, boots. Since court hearings in this rural county were about as informal as they could get most people including John came as they were.

This same laid back approach to the courts was practiced by all except me. While I did not dress formally except for trials I did change from my normal farm appearance into something more practical for a court. Many times I was the "best" dressed person in the courtroom.

Doshia Webb, the magistrate, was always casual. Tony dressed even more comfortably, but this was because of his immunological disease. Once he even had to wear pajamas because his skin was so inflamed. But on another occasion when I had stopped in his office before a hearing he actually had on a short sleeved, collared shirt. I egged him a little by inquiring why he was not wearing a tie. As if to show me that he could be spiffy he pulled out of his office closet the most vibrant, yellow tie and put it on.

So while John's appearance might have been a point of scrutiny in other courthouses, in Marlinton, West Virginia no one even noticed.

This was to change, however, when he accompanied me to the West Virginia Supreme Court of Appeals. Yes, John did wear clothing more up-beat than anything he wore in Marlinton, but he still had on that mountain hat and his boots. Both were wonderful offsets to the suits worn by all those lawyers who filled the courtroom and to my own dressed appearance.

I loved it when John and I sat in the front row of seats just opposite the justices. John's boots still had some mud and probably some manure on them from his morning feeding of his animals. Seeing us sitting together the justices immediately knew that they were going to hear a very special case. I could even feel the energy coming from them as their body language seemed to say that if these two guys were together it would be impossible to rule against me.

Chapter 11

I whistle a happy tune
And ev'ry single time
The happiness in the tune
Convinces me that I'm not afraid.

THE BENCH TRIAL

Prior to my first trial I informed the court and Tony Tatano, the prosecutor, that I thought my defense would take a couple of days. I had subpoenaed the director of the DNR, Frank Jezioro, Captain Mike Pizzino of the DNR and Howard Shinaberry one of the DNR conservation officers for Pocahontas County. The state would have conservation officer Duffield who filed the complaint and both Stoots and Harvey who had rescued the fawn, that by this time I had named Aspen.

Tony did step in and demanded a hearing to quash my subpoena of the DNR Director. It should be noted that Tony Tatano, Assistant Prosecutor for Pocahontas County was also the personal, private lawyer for the Judge, Doshia Webb.

The trial would be a "bench" trial meaning that Doshia Webb, the magistrate, would decide the case. I had been denied a jury trial. And by this time Doshia was not about to begin a Joel Rosenthal fan club. She openly felt and thought from all my motions and attempts to represent myself that I was "abusing" the system. In her mind this concept was reinforced by the fact that I enjoyed every minute of what was happening. At times she even alluded to this "attitude" of mine.

Wishing to have my own audio record of the trial, I brought on May 10th 2006 a tape recorder to the court. Behind my seat on the wall was an electric outlet. I plugged in my recorder and set in on the desk in front of me. I had lots of 90 minute cassette tapes and did not anticipate any kind of difficulty or conflict over wanting to tape the proceedings. I even thought that Doshia would be required to tape the trial so that my own taping would not be anything out of the ordinary. Much to my surprise Doshia not only forbade me from using my tape recorder, but acknowledged that she would not be taping the trial either. And because this was just an "insignificant" case in magistrate court no human court recorder would be used. This revelation that there would be no record of what took place for my case was a disturbing and disheartening.

To reinforce her feelings about the case she began the trial by telling me that she knew I was guilty, but that she would "allow" me to try to defend myself. "No wonder she did not want anything recorded," I thought.

In any criminal trial, theoretically, but also technically and legally, it is the burden of the State to "prove" its case against the defendant, me, beyond a reasonable doubt. At the very least I thought that I could instill lots of doubt.

Because of this burden on the State to "prove" its case, the prosecutor, Tony Tatano, had to present his case first to the court so that I, the defendant, could listen to any evidence against me and respond. Each side got to use its witnesses or evidence to reinforce its position. The State also had to use as a witness the officer who filed the complaint so that the defendant could face and examine his accuser. And of course since I was the defendant I could also put myself on the witness stand, but was not obligated to do so. Each witness could be cross examined by the other side. Witnesses would be sworn to tell the truth. If a witness did not tell the truth this would be considered perjury. Perjury in court was itself a separate crime.

My strategy was to use the State's witnesses as though they were my own. I would ask them questions for which I knew the answers. I had heard before that a lawyer should never ask a question to which he did not know the answer. A good lawyer also asks questions of witnesses such that no matter how they answer they will either be agreeing with the lawyer or will be easily impeached by the next question or another witness.

Stoots and Harvey were the first witnesses for the State. Tony simply asked them to tell what happened when they brought the fawn to me. Harvey said I had taken the fawn from them and put it in the front seat of my truck with Kip, my dog, and took a picture through the open door of the truck. I had sent a copy of this picture to the two guys via e-mail. Since both of them had already been convicted of the illegal possession of this fawn, I thought they might be a little reluctant to "help" the state, but I was wrong. Almost with glee they told the entire story of not only bringing me the fawn, but then pulled out the picture of Aspen in the front seat with Kip. Since I had never denied having the fawn, I presented to the court the same picture in color.

There really was nothing that I disputed which these fellows said, but of course Tony tried to limit their testimony to the fact that they gave me the fawn. When I had a chance to cross examine them I brought out how they had called the DNR, that the DNR did not take possession of the fawn, that the DNR told them to release it back into the wild, that this would have violated a cruelty to animal statute in WV and that indeed by bringing it to me, they and I fulfilled the "order" from the DNR. Therefore, since I was not the one who rescued the fawn and was only doing what the DNR had "ordered," I could not be guilty of a crime.

This examination and cross examination of the fellows who brought me Aspen took a few hours. In a way I was proud of myself from the standpoint that I did not let Tony run roughshod over me. I had already known that Doshia was going to rule against me so in a way everything was open and ironically I could relax more. Before the next witness could be called, Doshia declared it to be lunch time. I told the court that I had no further questions for Stoots and Harvey so they could go home 80 miles away.

I asked Tony what he was going to do for lunch and he told me that he was going to go to "The River Place," a restaurant perched right on the Greenbrier River on the other side of town. I told him I wanted to chat some more about the case and would accompany him there. At the restaurant another lawyer, the public defender, was already in a booth so we joined him. I was not really hungry and just ordered a drink.

To my amazement Doshia came into the restaurant a few moments later with all three of the DNR witnesses. Together they also sat down at a booth. As naïve as I was about the law, to me this was clearly another conflict of interest. How could the judge in my case in the middle of the trial engage in such blatant fraternity and camaraderie with my accusers? Had I known all of this was going to occur I would have brought a stuffed kangaroo to the courtroom for the afternoon session. But I really had to chuckle at the way "justice" was being administered in Pocahontas County.

My education of how things worked was further enhanced when Tony after finishing his meal suddenly "discovered" what he called a small gnat on the edge of his plate. In my mind I simply thought this to be insignificant and put this finding in the "so what" category. But Tony to my surprise called over the waitress and made a fuss about this gnat until she offered to forgive the bill for the meal. Pleased with his success at having suckered the restaurant out of payment for his lunch Tony then turned to me.

It seems that he now wanted to "reward" the waitress with a tip, but lo and behold he had no money. For some really crazy reason I loaned him five dollars to leave as a tip. No shyster on the street corner of any big city could have pulled off this double scam more efficiently than Tony Tatano, Assistant Prosecutor for Pocahontas County. I never again saw my five dollars.

By now I was really scratching my head. I had always thought that it was easy to pick out the "good" guys from the "bad" guys. Gosh was I getting an education.

We returned to the courtroom where the case reconvened with Her Honor, Magistrate, Doshia Webb, presiding. With all that had happened already at my motion hearings and now with only a half a day of my trial I knew that my only recourse was to try to have as much fun as possible in order to maintain my sanity. My fate in this court had been sealed weeks earlier and simply confirmed during the first few hours of the trial.

The afternoon session opened with Tony calling Shane Duffield to the stand. Even though he was the officer who filed the charge against me he really knew nothing about the case. Tony attempted to make him look knowledgeable on the stand, but it was obvious he could offer little.

With my cross examination I attempted to discredit Shane and to be as thorough as possible. This was easy since he had initially entered Point of View Farm property illegally. A part of the very Code 20-2-4 with which he charged me stated that any illegally possessed wildlife **"shall be forfeited."** Under my questioning he had to admit that he not only did not confiscate any wildlife, but that he never saw any fawn nor did he know for sure, when he came to my place, if I even had a fawn.

I also got him to admit that the DNR had no mechanism for dealing with an orphan animal except to kill it. Other admissions included the fact that throughout the year he authorized citizens to possess wildlife out of season when he allowed them to kill deer or bears, that indeed if I followed an "order" from the DNR to put the fawn back in the wild I could not be committing a crime and that he reported that I had this fawn four weeks before it was born. This latter fact he tried to correct earlier with a motion of his own. That motion was accepted even though it contained errors that I pointed out. The prosecutor even had the gall to say that Duffield putting down a false date for the alleged crime was simply a "harmless" error. This hubris on the part of the State would work against them later. But of course Magistrate Webb went along with it.

I grilled Shane on what he knew about the Constitution, about my telling him that I took care of fawns when he had visited in the past and about other mechanisms of "authorizations" to possess wildlife. I also got him to recognize that even with a hunting license one did not have to kill animals, but could capture and possess them alive. Ironically, all of his answers to my questions supported the quest for exoneration which I knew Doshia would never grant.

This interrogation from both Tony and me took another few hours. At one point Tony even objected to my method of questioning Officer Duffield claiming that I was badgering him. Of course I found this interesting because Shane Duffield was an experienced officer having worked previously as a town policeman. He was used to being in court and answering tough questions. Tony's attempts to rattle me only worked to my advantage. The more maneuvers he threw at me the more experience I got. How I dealt with these methods of his was key to how I learned to handle myself.

Once I finished cross examining Duffield, Tony "rested" the State's case as he had no more witnesses. Technically, I was instructed to put on my defense. In reality all of the witnesses used by the State were my witnesses, too. But I had also subpoenaed a couple other DNR officers.

I asked the bailiff to bring in Officer Howard Shinaberry who was supposed to be sequestered outside the courtroom. She went into the hallway to find him, but he was not there. It turns out that Howard decided that he did not feel well and went home. He did not even inform the court. Doshia was actually upset, but I believe she felt this way because she did not know what had happened. Howard just left without telling her. I made a motion for a mistrial or at least a recess until Howard could be returned or brought in another day. This did not sit well with her so she denied my motion and simply declared that the trial would continue without him. She even had the temerity to ask me if I really needed him. I think I just laughed because the entire case was rigged and her ludicrous comment just hit my funny bone.

Well, I did have another witness in Mike Pizzino, the Captain of our district of the DNR. It was at Mike Pizzino's office in Elkins, WV that the call came in from Pete Treadway about my getting the fawn. Howard Shinaberry happened to be there at the time and that is why he drove straight from Elkins to my place. Howard then entered the property without a warrant and without my being there. Later that week I talked to Howard on the phone. He not only admitted to all of these activities, but I tape recorded the conversation with him.

In West Virginia the law states that telephone conversations can be recorded as long as one of the participants knows about the recording. Law enforcement still has to have the court's permission to record private conversations. Since I tape recorded my conversation with Howard where he admitted to violating my Constitutional rights. I really wanted him as my witness, but this was not to be. So without Howard, Captain Pizzino would have to do.

When I bought the farm in 2000 it had been owned by two older men, Leonard Walker and John Fahey. They had owned it for the prior fifteen years. Neither one ever lived permanently on the property. John Fahey had been a forester in West Virginia and knew Leonard Walker who had been a wildlife biologist. Their purchase of the farm had been mostly for speculation. Leonard loved the land and indeed spent his summers living in the log cabin on the property. During the fall, winter and spring Leonard returned home to live with his family in Georgia. It was natural that the two of them would become acquainted with and become friends with Mike Pizzino. All of them enjoyed hunting and there was no better spot in all of West Virginia than this farm. Mike Pizzino, therefore, became very familiar with my property and hunted on it often prior to my making the purchase.

Interestingly, this also lead to another link to Pete Treadway. Since no one lived on the property during much of the year, Pete took it upon himself to trespass and hunt at his leisure, at almost any time and with disregard to hunting seasons. This was confirmed by both Mike and Doshia, both of whom had been DNR officers for the area. Doshia even fondly recalled the times she would "catch" Pete poaching game on the property when neither Leonard nor John was around.

Mike Pizzino was at the time of the trial about 55 years old and a long time veteran of the DNR. His promotion to Captain was as high as he would get. In a way he was just marking time through the next decade so that he could retire. Tall and lanky Mike actually looked quite spiffy in his olive green uniform.

To say Mike was a reluctant witness for me would be a huge understatement. In my mind law enforcement officers are taught and trained to remember situations down to the smallest detail. Mike had been such an officer for about 30 years. Yet, with almost all of my questions he just could not remember what had happened. He did not even recall my phone call to him a few days after getting Aspen. Interestingly, he could not even recall my admitting I had the fawn. I asked him about receiving the call from Pete, about his sending Howard to my place, about his knowledge of the U.S. Constitution and the requirements of obtaining a search warrant to enter a property, about the wording of WV Codes 20-2-4, 61-8-19 and 20-2C-1h, about why Shane Duffield was transferred to the "case," about his knowledge of my property, if anyone had ever been charged with the crime of helping a fawn and about why I was charged. At 55 years old it seemed he had developed amnesia.

With Magistrate Doshia Webb complicity Mike Pizzino dodged almost every question with non-committal, evasive or lack of memory answers. And as with Shane Duffield when I asked questions demanding a simple yes or no answer Doshia allowed him to ramble incoherently. The only concession I obtained was that I was charged "because I was uncooperative by throwing Shane Duffield off the property because he did not have a warrant." So despite the couple of hours Mike was on the stand and all the diversionary answers, he finally provided this his most important answer. I had been charged because as a citizen I had stood up to Officer Duffield and had exercised my Constitutional rights.

Tony performed his perfunctory cross examination which simply amounted to the anticipated condemnation of me.

With no other witnesses or any reexaminations of the witnesses on hand closing arguments began. Here the process is that the State puts on its closing arguments first, followed by the defense and then the State is able to address and try to refute anything said by the defense.

By this time though, the day was on the wane. We were approaching 6 PM and Doshia was determined that this trial would not run into another day. To me she and

Tony were obviously frustrated that they were not already in their homes enjoying an evening cocktail or dinner.

Tony again told the court that I had violated the law plain and simple. He went through his "evidence."

I then tried to bring up the many reasons I was not guilty. I wanted at least to once again put forth each of the legal reasons I was not only innocent, but authorized to care for the fawn. As I elaborated on each point Doshia would cut me off and tell me to move on to the next point. This went on for quite a while. It was obvious she did not want to hear anymore, but I pressed on. Finally, as she shortened each of my attempts to talk, I ran out of arguments and told her that since she would not let me close my case I had nothing more to say. Without even giving Tony a chance for his last rebuttal she slammed down her gavel and pronounced me guilty. Still standing as I had been since lunch I thanked her. And with one last remark she pronounced her sentence, a fine of 50 dollars plus 160 dollars in court costs.

Not wishing to leave the court house with unfinished business I insisted that she and I go into the Magistrate office so that I could pay her and to fill out any forms necessary to appeal her decision in circuit court.

Chapter 12

To dream the impossible dream
To fight the unbeatable foe

CONVICTION I

Well, I was now a convicted criminal. And while this result was little more than what one might get for driving through a stop sign for me it was highly significant. I had been convicted of a violation of the possession of wildlife. Caring for wildlife is what I did and if this conviction remained I might be prohibited from conducting other wildlife activities. But from another standpoint I had achieved much success. I for sure learned something about the law and how it was administered in Pocahontas County, WV. I learned how all the "actors" in such a public arena conducted themselves. I learned how Tony and the State presented the case and most important of all I learned how to handle myself in a court setting. I was no longer scared or intimidated by being in court.

Magistrate court, though, was just the first step toward my quest for true justice. Another interesting aspect of the law is that when you lose in one court you can still play again in another court. This is not so with many other endeavors. In sports for instance when you get to the playoffs you go home if you lose. Even the founders of our judicial system fully realized that our courts could be imperfect and make mistakes that needed further scrutiny by a higher audience.

In West Virginia the process of fully appealing court decisions is actually one less step than in many other states. Because my case was a criminal conviction I could appeal as far as I wanted through the court system, but according to the 5th amendment of the U.S. Constitution if I was to be exonerated the State could not appeal that decision. It is a protection against double jeopardy. In the West Virginia Constitution this protection is embodied in Article III Section 5. Following a conviction in magistrate court any appeal would next be heard by a judge in the 11th Circuit Court. This court embraced two counties, Pocahontas and Greenbrier County to the south. Two judges alternated cases. Both judges had offices in each courthouse, but they "resided" in the courthouse in the town of Lewisburg in Greenbrier County fifty miles to the south of Marlinton.

In many states the next step in any appeal following circuit court is to a higher appellate court and from there to the state Supreme Court. By having a state appellate court many cases are fully adjudicated at this point allowing the Supreme Court to handle the more persistent cases. In West Virginia, however, cases appealed from circuit court go directly to the West Virginia Supreme Court of Appeals. Clerks for the Supreme Court Justices screen the cases making crucial decisions about which ones the Court will actually hear. But, even with this culling process the West Virginia Supreme Court of Appeals hears more cases than just about any other State Supreme Court in the country. Of course depending on the particulars of any case appeals based on U.S. Constitutional grounds can still be made to the Federal District Court and then possibly to the United States Supreme Court.

My appeal to Circuit Court included all the motions for dismissal that I submitted to Magistrate Court. They included: no criminal intent, authorization by my business license, authorization by the DNR when they ordered the fawn released back into the environment, statutes in *pari materia* 20-2-4 and 61-8-19, selective prosecution, *estoppels* by silence, statute in *desuetude*, errors in the summons and complaint, illegally deprived of a jury trial, authorization by cruelty to animals statute 61-8-19 and authorization by my non-profit status via WV Statute 20-2C-1h. Since I had brought all of these issues before the Magistrate Court I was entitled to use them in my appeal.

The type of appeal one can have in Circuit Court depends on the type of trial one had in Magistrate Court. In a criminal case if one had a bench trial (one decided only by the judge and not a jury) then the appeal is heard by the Circuit Court judge as a trial de novo, a new trial. If the appeal to Circuit Court is from a conviction by jury in Magistrate Court then the hearing in Circuit Court is based on the record from the Magistrate Court. Since Doshia did not tape record my bench trial and did not allow me to record it, theoretically, any full hearing on the matter in Circuit Court would have to be a totally new bench trial. The new judge could not make a ruling on the "facts" of the Magistrate Court trial since none would be available.

As a part of my petition for appeal and the submission of my motions I requested a hearing before the Circuit Court Judge, but first I had to deal with a medical difficulty.

I had developed pain in my back and legs over the past year. I had thought it was just a residual condition from the muscle difficulties I had experienced from taking Lipitor, a cholesterol lowering drug. For a while I could hardly walk from the muscle spasms. Six months earlier after doing some internet research on Lipitor. I just quit using the drug cold turkey. Improvement occurred slowly, but was noticeable. I no longer developed the knotting and pain in my muscles. But now pain had radiated into my lower back.

A physical examination, X rays and an MRI revealed stenosis to my lower vertebrae and a slight slippage of a disc. This clogging of the channel through my lumbar region put pressure on the nerves leading to my pain and discomfort. An operation was scheduled for that summer. Recovery time would delay my ability to appear in court, but I had already realized that a full adjudication of my case could take a very long time. I was in no rush.

As part of my defense I had decided that Governor Joe Manchin, Jr. III would be an excellent witness for me. He had previously been the Secretary of State for West Virginia and had signed my business license and issued to me a Certificate of Authority to conduct my business activities to care for abandoned and needy wildlife. Surely he would testify that I was authorized to possess wildlife.

The Honorable Frank Joliffe would be the Circuit Court Judge for my appeal. I received an "order" from him where he acknowledged having received all of my motions and subpoenas and set a date for the hearing. In his "order" he specifically noted my assertion that I had been illegally denied a jury trial and said that he would deal with this first. In that motion I had based my claim on two main issues. The first was that Magistrate Beverage who administered my arraignment had failed to tell me I only had 20 days to file a specific request for a jury. The other issue was that when Shane Duffield had filed a motion to correct the date of my alleged crime, the case in essence should have begun again from scratch (de novo) allowing me to once more request a jury. The other matter that Judge Joliffe would deal with was a motion from the West Virginia Attorney General's office to quash my subpoena to have Governor Manchin as my witness.

I should state here that each of my motions for dismissal included the request that they be accepted with prejudice. I had always been a little confused by this term, but what it meant was that if a case either criminal or civil were to be dismissed before trial with prejudice then neither the State in a criminal case nor the plaintiff in a civil case could ever again re-file that case. For me that would mean that a judge ruling on the merits of my motions would essentially exonerate me. If a case was dismissed without prejudice then either the State or a plaintiff could re-file the case if it corrected any deficiencies that the court defined. Situations like this may develop if a procedure was not followed. A dismissal without prejudiced on this basis in a civil case, thus, allowed the plaintiff to correct and follow the procedure when re-filing the case. Rarely is a case dismissed without prejudice in a criminal case. Usually, the State is simply allowed to correct its error. This was demonstrated when Shane Duffield was allowed to correct the date on his complaint where he erroneously claimed I had possessed the fawn before it was born. I argued for a dismissal with prejudice. I argued that this was essentially a re-filing of the case since the complaint had been modified such that my defense was modified.

Tony Tatano to my surprise was forced by my motions to file lengthy responses in writing to Judge Joliffe. In some ways it is impossible to describe my joy at having him attempt to counter all my motions, subpoenas and filings to the Circuit Court. With page after page after page he tried to mitigate or refute my motions and subpoenas. I was ecstatic. Once again I learned that anytime I as the defendant could get the prosecutor, the State, the judge, the Attorney General's office or anyone involved in the case to make any written statement it would be to my advantage. Invariably they would make mistakes giving me a greater opportunity to impeach the state's case.

At our hearing Judge Joliffe first dealt with my subpoena for the Governor to be my witness. To my astonishment another lawyer, Christine Utt, from the Attorney General's office in Charleston drove three hours to the Marlinton courthouse to quash my subpoena. Another coup for me, I thought. I knew I may never win my case, but for sure I was getting the education of my life on the way the system worked. I had no lawyer so I had no major costs. Even subpoenas I learned did not have to be served by a process server which cost $25 each. By this method one first asked the clerk of the court to type a subpoena and then paid the clerk the $25 to have an official person, the process server, hand carry the subpoena to the targeted person, hand the subpoena to that person, fill out a form stating that the subpoena had been served and then return the form to the clerk. The law, however, did not require this level of sophistication for serving a subpoena. About the only restriction was that the subpoena could not be served directly (by hand) by the person requesting it. Any other adult citizen could serve a subpoena and simply fill out the form that the subpoena had been given to the recipient. When local persons were to be served this second method could be used with zero cost. But a third more cost-time efficient method that could be used simply involved sending the subpoena via registered mail with a receipt signature request. Since bureaucrats in Charleston, the capital of West Virginia, were often difficult to track down even subpoenas delivered by a process server would often be signed by the office receptionist. By sending subpoenas via registered mail the same end result could be achieved. Subpoenas, though, were technically only valid for the listed date of the court appearance. Should a hearing be continued or changed to another date a new subpoena needed to be issued unless a request is included with the original subpoena that the recipient of the subpoena be notified of any changes in the dates of appearance.

It was now more than a year since I had gotten Aspen. During this time I had made dozens of court appearances, filed dozens of motions, sent Tony and Walt many letters and of course had been convicted by Doshia in an eight hour trial in Magistrate Court of one count of the illegal possession of wildlife. My total costs were almost nothing. I could not truly imagine what the entire process so far had cost the State of West Virginia in the hundreds of hours employees of law enforcement and the justice system had to invest and of direct monetary costs. It had to be many, many thousands of dollars; perhaps a hundred thousand dollars or more.

At Judge Joliffe's hearing I would learn another interesting fact. Judges, if possible, will take the easiest path to minimize their involvement in a case. Christine Utt was asked why she wished my subpoena for the Governor to be quashed. Basically, she said that the Governor was not involved in the case and had no information which could be useful. The judge then asked me why I wanted the Governor as a witness. I told him about the Governor's previous job as Secretary of State in West Virginia and how in that capacity he signed and issued me a Certificate of Authority to conduct my business and that I wanted him to testify in that capacity. Of course I also wanted the Governor to testify that he read my application for a business license and had determined that my business activity conformed to law.

In reality I knew, the prosecutor knew, Christine Utt knew and the judge knew that the Secretary of State in West Virginia did not read any applications for business licenses. Others in his office handled this task. The Secretary of State did not even actually sign his own name to the Certificate of Authority. The document was either stamped with the Secretary's signature or someone else signed for him. More important, though, is the fact that the State of West Virginia represents the signature to be authentic. And the last thing the State wanted was for the Governor to appear in court, swear to tell the truth and then be asked questions about his role in issuing to Point of View Farm, Inc. the business license and the Certificate of Authority. Such an interrogation could be very embarrassing if the Governor told the truth and perjury if he lied. I knew this, Tony knew this, Christi Utt knew this and the judge knew this. It was therefore the "duty" of the judge to protect the Governor. Judge Joliffe, therefore, in a way to "satisfy" all parties simply declared that the court would accept the fact that my Certificate of Authority was indeed signed by Governor Manchin and agreed to quash my subpoena.

Judge Joliffe then directed his attention to my motion claiming I had been illegally denied a jury trial. I had hoped he would have first dismissed my case with prejudice by acting on any or all of my motions to that effect. Obviously, had he done this first there would have been no reason to even care about my having a jury. But, as I found out he took what seemed like the easy way out. He ruled that indeed when the state amended its complaint against me to change the date I received the fawn, it should have dismissed the case without prejudice and re-filed the case. This then would have offered me the opportunity to file the necessary papers for a jury trial. And the judge opined that the action of changing the summons constituted a case *de novo* for which I was entitled to file for a jury trial. He, thus, remanded or sent the case back to Magistrate Court and Doshia Webb for a new trial, giving me the opportunity to request a jury trial and to practice again my court acumen.

Since I was to get another trial I had to approach it from the standpoint that I had never had a trial. This meant not only formally filing the request for a jury, but it meant filing all those motions again and making all the same requests as before. Of course I already had the material in my computer so it was just a matter of changing the case number and dates on the Certificates of Service, making new copies and giving them to the same people all over again.

Chapter 13

To bear with unbearable sorrow
To run where the brave dare not go

THE JURY TRIAL

With this new trial now in the same court with the same players, ahead of me Tony, the prosecutor, decided to include an additional strategy against me: "The threat of Chronic Wasting Disease"

There is a disease called Chronic Wasting Disease that affects deer and indeed many of the Cervix (deer) family. Affected animals develop a general wasting of body tissues, the brain is affected and the animal finally dies. Of particular interest is that the disease is caused by a protein devoid of any nucleic acids like DNA, deoxyribonucleic acid or RNA, ribonucleic acid which are the molecules that control the genetic functions of every cell in the body. Recognition that a protein could be infectious and reproduce itself inside body cells, cause disease and death was of great concern. It was also shown that these proteins were resistant to many chemical treatments usually used to disarm infectious organisms.

These proteins were called prions. From the standpoint of our human understanding of them our knowledge was relatively new. Indeed some animals and even some humans showed for a long time similar signs of degeneration and death that could not be explained, but it was not until about 50 years ago that scientists began to unravel the mystery.

In humans it was of considerable interest to find that some of the people of certain tribes in Papua, New Guinea developed a brain degeneration and death following the custom of eating the brains of their dead. In these tribes the symptoms were called Kuru. Similar manifestations in other humans were described in people with Creutzfeldt-Jakob disease (CJD).

In sheep and goats it had been known for a long time that some animals would also develop a degenerative brain disease and die. Experiments showed that these symptoms called Scrapie could be transferred in laboratories from sheep to mice despite the fact that no organism or virus could be detected. A similar disease was also found in mink. The name of Transmissible Spongiform Encephalopathy (TSE) was finally given to the phenomena describing what happened to the brain.

A similar disease in cattle has been called Mad Cow Disease or Bovine Spongiform Encephalopathy (BSE). BSE was detected in the mid-1980s and has received a great deal of concern for its possible relationship to the human disease (CJD) and because so much of humanity eats cattle and cattle products.

In cervids this disease called Chronic Wasting Disease (CWD) had been observed for about 30 years. Four species, mule deer, moose, elk and white tailed deer, are known to be susceptible.

Transmission of the TSE diseases has been shown to be by contact with infected animal parts and wastes. For quite some time many domestic animals had been given feeds whose protein content was enhanced with other animal parts. Prior to this only vegetable protein was used in feeds. It is thus thought that an increase in BSE in cattle is a direct result of some animals being feed infected protein. A concomitant increase in the incidence of CJD in humans has been attributed to the possibility of humans eating infected cattle products.

With this as a background it is prudent for every wildlife agency in the country to be concerned about the spread of Chronic Wasting Disease especially in whitetail deer since this is the most hunted mammal in North America. Not only could the populations of whitetail deer be threatened, but the relationship to human disease for those who eat and handle cervid products is of great concern.

In May of 2005 when I received Aspen no Chronic Wasting Disease had been detected in West Virginia. As a matter of fact no Chronic Wasting Disease had even been detected in any adjacent states to West Virginia. Because of this deer harvested via hunting at any place in West Virginia could be transported to any other place in West Virginia and the waste parts discarded as one wished. Likewise the many game farms in West Virginia that raised deer could buy, sell or exchange live animals with any other like farmer without any regulation or concern. Since Aspen had been rescued about 80 miles from me I had no concern about this fawn disseminating any kind of disease.

By the end of 2005 this all changed in that the West Virginia DNR reported it had detected Chronic Wasting Disease in a couple of deer that had been shot during hunting season that fall. The cases had been confined to one county in the north-ern part of the state. No one could say how or why this had happened. Maryland, Pennsylvania and Ohio, other states in the same proximate geographical area, had still not reported any such disease. The mystery of the source of this CWD continues to this day.

In 2006, at the time of my second trial, knowledge about this outbreak of CWD in northern West Virginia was well known. And indeed the WV DNR had initiated some regulations about which deer products could be transported around the state from hunted deer.

Tony, the prosecutor, now decided to try to make a point of the risks of moving animals from one part of the state to another and of course he wanted to use CWD as his poster child. From this framework he decided that he would tell the jury that by taking a fawn from another part of the state I violated prudent biological practices and indeed put at jeopardy the wildlife of West Virginia. In order to attempt to give some validity and credence to this concept he via discovery informed me that he was going to subpoena the state's chief biologist, a Dr. James Crum, as his expert witness.

At first I was somewhat concerned by this move of Tony's because Dr. Crum would surely give credence to the dangers of moving any animal around the state. However, upon some reflection I decided that dealing with Tony's "move" would not only be fun, but that I could channel any of these efforts to my own advantage.

I had spent almost two decades of my life as a scientist and biologist working for the U.S. government. I had worked with many viruses and knew of the diseases caused by prions. I had even spent some time with Dr. Carlton Gadjusek, a Nobel Prize winner for his work in New Guinea with Kuru. Not only was I sure Tony knew absolutely nothing about Chronic Wasting Disease or other infectious spongiform encephalopathies, but I was pretty certain I knew more than Dr. Crum. In my mind if Tony was really going to try to put Doctor Crum on the stand I thought that I could expose his lack of knowledge about Chronic Wasting Disease and about prions. Besides I knew that a more interesting "ace" in the hole was that my case had nothing to do with moving animals around the state or even about CWD. In court, "objections" are often lodged demanding that the other side show "relevance." When I got Aspen there were absolutely no rules, regulations or statutes against transporting animals within West Virginia. I was only being charged with illegal possession, nothing else.

By the time I was through thinking about Dr. Crum, I was actually looking forward to dealing with him. But first I had to take care of two tasks. One was to obtain enough documentation about infectious spongiform encephalitis diseases to overwhelm Tony. The second was to file a motion to prohibit Tony from even using Dr. Crum as a witness. If I did not object to Dr. Crum being an expert witness then I could not use his testimony as a part of any appeal I might need to file later.

I assembled my stack of information on infectious spongiform encephalopathies and gave them to Tony telling him that I looked forward to making a fool out of his "expert" witness and that I did not think that he, Tony, could formulate intellectually, astute enough questions to even make any sense. I also filed my motion challenging the relevance of any testimony Dr. Crum could possibly provide. It was simple I told the court. I was charged with the illegal possession of wildlife, not with moving wildlife across the state, which was not a crime anyway. Dr. Crum was not a law enforcement officer, was not a witness to any of the actions in regards to the fawn, was not an expert in the law or in the statutes of WV and knew nothing about the case. Testimony he might make in regards to Chronic Wasting Disease was totally irrelevant since CWD was not even known in WV at the time the fawn was brought to me. As usual Magistrate Webb rejected my motion.

On the morning of the jury trial date I dressed in a much more spiffy fashion than I had for my other more mundane motion hearings. Proceedings carried out in the courtrooms of the Pocahontas County Court house are pretty laid back and casual. I have never seen any magistrate dress in anything other than normal daily home attire. And, never did any of them wear black robes. The courthouse was so relaxed that both Tony and Doshia often brought their dogs to work. Interestingly, my dog, Kip, a border collie, never wanted to leave my side so on every visit to town and to the court house Kip would ride in the truck with me. If Tony and Doshia had their dogs in the courthouse I would bring in Kip. When I watched other trials, very rarely did a defendant or witnesses wear anything more than their normal daily attire. Lawyers representing clients on the other hand would always appear in a suit and tie. For all my "normal" hearings I put on clean clothes, a nice pair of slacks and an appropriate shirt. But for my "normal" trips to town I simply wore the "farm" clothes of boots, jeans and a raggedy shirt I had on every day.

For Circuit Court which was held in the courtroom on the top floor of the court-house both my and Tony's dress reflected a greater "respect" for the court. I had on slacks and a sport jacket, Tony a long sleeved shirt and a tie. Judges wore their black robes, bailiffs called the court to order and a court reporter tapped out the proceedings as well as recording them on tape. However, Magistrate Webb always appeared in Circuit Court wearing her same kaki work pants, work shoes and a long sleeved shirt.

I was now experienced enough to proceed at least with the confidence that I thought I knew what I was doing. Of course dealing with a jury would be a new experience. I discovered that as a defendant I had rights in regards to what would be told to the jurors as part of their instructions. I had been provided a list of potential jurors from which six would be selected to serve during the trial. I also had the right to have them answer some questions about any prejudices they might have or even about their thoughts about various topics. From their answers I could request that the court exclude or strike any particular juror. I also had the right to strike any juror preemptively for no reason at all. Tony as the prosecutor for the State also had these rights.

Prospective jurors are chosen from the voting rolls in the county. Since Poca-hontas County had less than 9,000 residents I figured that I might actually know some of those on the prospective jury list presented to me. And while each juror had to promise that they would judge the case on the facts presented at trial and not on personalities or other factors the reality is that we are all human and as such human factors could play a role. Tony had lived in the county for his entire adult life and as such knew far more people than I did, but I did not believe anyone would vote against me just because they knew Tony. On the other hand a charge of the illegal posses-sion of wildlife usually meant that someone shot or killed an animal out of season. I was being charged with saving a fawn. My hope would be that the jurors would see the situation for what it was and exercise a more prudent and pragmatic approach to whether I was a real criminal. Besides, the West Virginia Supreme Court had ruled in a previous decision that a jury could nullify a law if it found that the law was either vague or inapplicable or even if the jury just found that it did not believe the act applied.

In the "real" criminal world jury selection for high profile crimes is a science which is designed to take advantage of the human factors involved. One should never forget that a decision by a jury in a criminal trial to convict had to be unanimous. In my case that meant all six citizens would have to convict me. Surely I thought I could find one juror to vote for acquittal thus "hanging" the jury. Having all the jurors find in my favor, nevertheless, would be the goal. Should any jury simply be hung with only some of them ruling in favor of the defendant, the State and the prosecutor had the right to retry the case.

The jury list I was sent consisted of 14 names. I did recognize two of the people. My initial strategy was to simply keep lots of women on the jury figuring that they would be inclined to acquit someone who helped animals. I figured that males, here in Pocahontas County, would probably be hunters and would not care too much about a fawn.

I have to admit at this point that I was again somewhat torn between two concepts. One was that I wanted to win my case and be acquitted as soon as possible. But on the other hand being found innocent in Magistrate Court would not set a precedent. This meant that I could always be charged again for helping the next fawn or any other animal. If I could win on appeal in Circuit Court then my business license and charitable status would have clout and should prevent any charges in the future. In discussing this with John Leyzorek we both acknowledged that no matter what, I had to fight as hard as I could to be acquitted first in front of this jury.

Prior to the trial I submitted a motion to have the Magistrate read my version of the jury instructions. This consisted of a synopsis of about 20 statutes and court rulings. One of them was the WV Supreme Court ruling that indeed a jury could nullify a law. Of course Tony objected and at a hearing Doshia sustained his objection saying that she would not read a statement that contained only parts of the statutes to the jury. I told her fine and that I would resubmit my motion so that I included the full texts of all the statutes in my request. This second motion was heard and of course Tony objected saying that the request was way too long and burdensome. Indeed it now contained over 50 pages I wanted read to the jury. Again in a defiant mood Doshia sustained Tony's objection and declared that she would read the jury instructions of her choosing and that would be that.

Court began at 9AM on the morning of the trial. The first order of business was to have a preliminary hearing. By statute this is supposed to be recorded by the Magistrate, but Doshia did not turn on the tape recorder. The purpose of the hearing was to make sure that any issues between the opposing parties that could be resolved would be done at this time. While the hearing was to be conducted by Magistrate Webb, in reality, she just seemed disinterested and unfocused at her desk less than 10 feet from us. Tony brought up the issue of whether I had any documents which I claimed gave me the authority to possess wildlife. I responded by reminding him of my business license and accompanying Certificate of Authority and of the rulings of the IRS when it granted Point of View Farm, Inc. status as a non- profit charity to set up an animal sanctuary to care for injured, orphaned and endangered animals. Tony playing the role of tough guy prosecutor asked to see these documents. Of course I reminded him that he had copies, but nevertheless I showed them to him again. And as usual in his inimitable way he simply rejected them as not being valid. Doshia whose duty it is to run the courtroom, make decisions and to be aware of what occurs said nothing, did nothing and seemed aware of nothing. Right in front of her, Tony and I began to argue about the validity of my documents. He kept asserting that I had not shown him anything which he would accept and I kept saying that the documents were signed by the current governor of West Virginia and by the United States Internal Revenue Service. Well, all of this farce finally ended. Tony told Doshia to simply proceed and that was that.

The next step was to bring in the jury and allow me and Tony to decide who would be eliminated and who would stay. Since I had recognized two of the jurors I decided to try to keep both of them. Most of the jurors were female, but I recognized one of the males whom I had seen at a couple of parties and had conversed with before. The other person I recognized was one of the females. This changed my strategy a little since now instead of wanting all ladies on the final jury I decided that I would try to keep the male I knew.

The jurors were asked the typical questions about their ability to render a fair and impartial verdict and whether they had any prejudices about the case against either the defendant or the DNR or the State. Tony and I then in an alternate manner excused two jurors each. Finally there were 7 jurors left and one had to be eliminated. The two jurors I knew were still there. One, the female volunteered that she knew me, but that she could hear the case in an impartial manner. Doshia asked each of us who would like to eliminate the last juror. We both said yes, but of course Doshia allowed

Tony to make the final decision. He eliminated the lady I knew. This left five ladies and the one guy I knew. I felt satisfied. As a matter of fact I felt very confident and to some extent even worried that I would easily win the case right there in magistrate court.

As with the bench trial Doshia, the magistrate, conducted and ruled on this trial. And while she did not record the pre-trial hearing as she should have, she did tape record the jury trial. The trial began with the State putting on its case against me.

Tony began by calling Shane Duffield to the stand. Shane was the DNR officer who filed the complaint against me. Tony hardly asked any questions and then allowed me to cross examine Officer Duffield. From the beginning I attempted to establish a time line of everything that happened by asking him questions about our previous relationship and about what he knew in regards to the law. With almost every question Shane either developed his convenient memory loss or was protected from answering basic questions by Tony making absolutely inane objections which were sustained. A perfect example of this was when I asked Shane Duffield questions as to if he knew of any mechanisms by which I could legally possess wildlife. Tony objected saying that he made a motion at the pre- trial hearing asking me for any authorization that I might have and that I produced nothing. I refuted this, but Doshia then stated that indeed she ruled against me in the pre-trial hearing. This was totally false in that she made no rulings at the hearing, did not record the hearing as required by law and was not even paying attention during the hearing. As a matter of fact she did not even know that I showed and gave Tony any documents.

Nevertheless, despite this obvious prejudice by Doshia I proceeded to question Shane about permissions to obtain wildlife. He also acknowledged that even a hunting license is not issued by any government agency, but by clerks in merchant stores and outdoor, sportsman businesses around the state. And he had no choice but to recognize that the very statute by which he charged me allowed for the possession of migratory birds via permits from the U.S. Fish and Wildlife Service, not the WV DNR. He also admitted and demonstrated that he did not understand that "hunting" did not necessarily mean a person had to kill an animal. Hunting could be to hunt and catch an animal and that simply possessing it for the duration of the hunting season was not illegal. I also asked him if he had any knowledge that I had any criminal intent in regards to possessing the fawn. He said that he did not know of my intent.

Since having criminal intent is a part of the law, Officer Duffield's admission that he did not know of my intent easily introduced the concept of doubt as to if I had committed any crime at all.

While I made a few more attempts to ask questions, Tony not only kept objecting, but testifying himself. As usual, Doshia did not know what to do so she asked me for the relevancy of my questions. I tried to tell her that the actions of the DNR itself constituted cruel and unusual punishment when Tony blurted out that he wanted a mistrial. I said fine. At this point Doshia should have declared a mistrial on the basis that both sides agreed on the request.

RULE 26.3 MISTRIAL
Before ordering a mistrial, the court shall provide an opportunity for the state and for each defendant to comment on the propriety of the order, including whether each party consents or objects to a mistrial, and to suggest any alternatives.
[Adopted effective September 1, 1995.]

Doshia, however, would not grant the request so we continued. Tony also made a statement that he would ask for me to be found in contempt of court if I continued my statements. While I knew that this "threat" by Tony was spurious and insane, I also knew that Doshia would do anything Tony asked so I tried to temper my comments.

The prosecutor and I then finished with Officer Duffield. Tony then called James Stoots, who was one of the fellows that had brought the fawn to me.

Tony immediately brought up the fact that this fellow had been charged with the illegal possession of wildlife for having the fawn in the first place. I immediately objected stating that he being charged was totally irrelevant and prejudicial to my case. Of course Doshia overruled my objection. Tony recreated the story of Stoots and Harvey bringing me the fawn and then turned the witness, Stoots, over to me.

I attempted to ask Mr. Stoots questions about his knowledge of the law and what happened at his trial. Tony objected saying his knowledge of the law was irrelevant. Of course to me this was a total irony in that it was Tony who brought up this matter of him being charged, but now would not let me ask him questions about his knowledge of the law. I finished and little was learned from this witness.

Tony then called as a witness Jonathan Shane Harvey, the other fellow who brought me the fawn. The usual questions followed until Tony got Mr. Harvey to say something about Chronic Wasting Disease of Deer (CWD).

Tony baited Mr. Harvey into this and I immediately objected saying not only was this part of the discussion irrelevant, but that no case of CWD as of May of 2005 had ever been found in West Virginia or in any adjacent state. But as usual my objection fell on Doshia's deaf ears.

When I finally got to question Harvey I tried to elucidate the facts about Chronic Wasting Disease, but Tony and I got into a real shouting match because Tony naturally objected to my questions because he did not want the information put into testimony.

In a way this part of the trial was fun because everything was so out of control. For about 15 minutes Tony and I shouted at each other, calling each other names and attacking each other. Doshia could not maintain order. She stumbled and bumbled and in a metaphoric way she simply disappeared, hiding under her desk till the smoke cleared. Little was accomplished except that I demonstrated that I would not be pushed around by this cabal of Tony and Doshia. Doshia definitely lost control of the court, but it was Tony, a lawyer and the prosecutor for Pocahontas County, who lost his cool more than anyone. I would not allow him to get away with all his illegal testimony. I am proud of my efforts.

Following Mr. Harvey's testimony I asked to have Shane Duffield brought back for a few more questions. I wanted to ask him about the segment of the statute which required that any illegally possessed wildlife be forfeited. This I did and in reality I thought that I made some important points when I got Duffield to admit that no one ever confiscated the fawn nor did I forfeit it to anyone. But again Tony and I got into one hellacious argument. The amazing thing is that while Doshia and Tony had been in court many hundreds of times it was I who benefited from these boisterous exchanges. For me it was easy to out think and out speak Tony. All Tony was doing was trying to prevent me from presenting the facts and evidence and by the court allowing us to yell and scream at each other I was able to put forth my positions. And for sure I was not going to yield to Tony, despite his position, title and degree. Toe to toe we exchanged our verbal blows.

Doshia finally asked me if I had any other witnesses. I had subpoenaed Captain Mike Pizzino, who was both Officer Duffield's and Officer Shinaberry's supervisor. But by this time I saw the handwriting on the wall in that the officers conveniently lost their memories. So instead I simply told the court that I wanted to put myself on the stand so that I could tell my story. This she assured me I could do without the necessity of having a lawyer ask me the questions.

Citizens are protected by the 5th Amendment of the U.S. Constitution against self-incrimination. No one charged with a criminal offense is required to say anything to an agent of the State. At trial such a suspect cannot be compelled to testify if he does not want to be a witness. And the jury is not supposed to infer any guilt from such a refusal. Usually, though, a suspect who can handle himself on the witness stand can at the very least tell his story about why he is innocent.

The Fifth Amendment to the United States Constitution is as follows:

No person shall be held to answer for a capital, or otherwise infamous crime, unless on a presentment or indictment of a Grand Jury, except in cases arising in the land or naval forces, or in the Militia, when in actual service in time of War or public danger; nor shall any person be subject for the same offence to be twice put in jeopardy of life or limb; nor shall be compelled in any criminal case to be a witness against himself, nor be deprived of life, liberty or property, without due process of law; nor shall private property be taken for public use, without just compensation.

On the witness stand I tried to be very polite and simply tell the jury who I was and what my business was and what I did. But of course Tony hardly let me get a few words out before he objected. He did not want me to say I ran an animal sanctuary. I countered by saying that my organization Point of View Farm, Inc. was incorporated, had a business license in West Virginia and was so designated by the U.S. Internal Revenue Service as an animal sanctuary. Tony would not let go as he hammered away that I had given him nothing that substantiated my claim. I was amazed because not only did he have all of this information from Discovery, but I had shown him the documents again at our pre-trial hearing. The man was flat out lying and Doshia was buying into his fabrications. From my place on the witness stand I could not control myself any longer and lashed out at him by telling everyone in the court that he was a miserable liar. At that point everything fell apart because I was not going to allow him to distort the truth in such a manner.

I would like to emphasize again that this courtroom was tiny. The entire room measured only 14 feet wide by 20 feet long. Because of this all the action and all of the people were squeezed into one short piece of this small rectangular room. The jury sat against one short wall of the rectangle. A few feet from them was situated the witness chair and judge's desk. Directly opposite her desk sat the prosecutor and to his left I had a chair. The room was hot, but a floor fan between the witness chair and the jurors kept a little air moving. The noise of the fan made hearing the words of witnesses difficult. Since I stood during the entire trial I tended to lean to my right, over and onto Tony who remained seated. Sometimes when I was questioning witnesses I almost smothered Tony. And yet all of us were within 10 feet of one another. To my left and against the other short wall were chairs for spectators and for the court bailiff, a uniformed, armed officer. Three of my friends, John Leyzorek, Norman Alderman and Dick Evans were in the room along with Drew Tanner who was the reporter for the weekly paper, the Pocahontas Times. Drew had followed my entire case and wrote many long articles about what was happening. All of this meant that 15 people were squeezed into a room of only 280 square feet, giving each person less than a four by five foot space for the entire day.

So at this point in the small, hot, claustrophobic room a verbal brawl had broken out between me and the prosecutor. In retrospect I feel so fortunate that my court experiences included both a judge and prosecutor playing such hard ball with me. Tony was pulling out all the stops and at times and I had to adjust very quickly without experience of his antics. But by his actions he was giving me valuable experience as to how low a prosecutor would go with his manipulations, distortions, prevarications, and commensurations with the judge.

As I write this I am listening to tape recordings of the trial, but it is amazing that Doshia actually turned off the tape machine during this critical exchange so there is no recording of this fight between me and Tony. To say Doshia had lost control would be an understatement.

I tried to present my evidence to Doshia and to the court, but Tony objected to everything and Doshia sustained his objections. I finally got her to admit that I indeed had a business license, but she would not allow me to submit it as evidence. I argued that I thought the jury should be able to read the document and my Certificate of Authority so that the jurors could make their own decision. She also refused to allow me to submit as evidence my paperwork from the IRS, which would confirm that I ran an animal sanctuary and could possess wildlife.

And when she returned to recording the trial again she flat out stated that she did not see me give Tony anything at the pre-trial hearing despite the fact that she was just a few feet in front of me when I gave him the documents.

I had hardly gotten past introducing myself to the jury when I had the knock down drag out fight with the prosecutor and the judge. Over and over I tried to present my documents and show where the law supported them. Over and over Tony successfully had Doshia reject my attempts at submitting even other statutes which supported my position. I then tried to relay to the jury what had occurred when Harvey and Stoots brought me the fawn. Immediately both Tony and Doshia declared that I could not repeat what these guys had testified, saying that this was hearsay. Their collusion on this matter could not have been more in error. Testimony given in a trial is not hearsay.

Doshia more and more was now just parroting what Tony said. The day was growing late. Five o'clock in the afternoon came and went. I could see everyone was tired and tired of me trying to defend myself. But I did not care. This was my opportunity to put everything on the record. I was not going to give in to them. I did not care if Doshia, Tony or the jury hated me; I was going to stand up for my rights even though Doshia would not allow me to deliver my statement of what happened.

I should note at this point that in West Virginia the case of State v. Boyd defined the role of the prosecutor as follows:

The prosecuting attorney occupies a quasi-judicial position in the trial of a criminal case. In keeping with this position, he is required to avoid the role of a partisan eager to convict, and must deal fairly with the accused as well as the other participants in the trial. It is the prosecutor's duty to set a tone of fairness and pursue the State's case, in so doing he must not abandon the quasi-judicial role with which he is cloaked under the law.

And in another case: **No. 25844 - State of West Virginia v. Walter Lee Swafford, II,** Justice Starcher of the WV Supreme Court similarly opined as above, but with more detail. .

Tony flagrantly violated all of the above with his distortions, lies, and personal association with the judge.

Since I was prevented from even testifying to my side of the story the witness phase of the trial ended.

Tony presented his closing and I followed.

I tried to reason with the jury about all the mechanisms by which I was authorized to possess wildlife. From the judge's own admission they know I had a business license and she would not allow them to see it. This alone I argued had to create doubt in their minds about my guilt. But when I tried to use the testimony of Shane Duffield, Tony objected, saying it was hearsay. In an "honest" court this ruse would not have been allowed, but Doshia once again sustained his objection.

Tony then finished the closing arguments with his usual dribble about how I was guilty.

The jury deliberated for about 45 minutes. With the announcement that they had reached a verdict the court was reconvened. Without fanfare the jury found me guilty.

Because of the late hour, Doshia postponed the sentencing phase till a later date and court was adjourned.

Later I asked "my friend" on the jury why they had voted to find me guilty. He replied that he had gotten a traffic ticket once and had to pay for it. Therefore, he figured I, too, should have to pay my "ticket." When I asked if the jury considered the facts or the concept that the State did not prove anything, he said "no."

To right the unrightable wrong
To love pure and chaste from afar

JUSTICE?

So that is how the jury system works in Pocahontas County and I presume most of the United States.

In reality it is a crap shoot. Many prosecutors do not care to see your evidence or will distort your testimony for their own prejudicial reasons. Judges, especially those who have a business relationship with the prosecutor, will blatantly rule against you even though they, themselves, have been a party to your actions in the past and a jury is simply a conglomeration of citizens most of whom are ignorant of the law and their responsibilities. Such is "justice" as administered in much of America.

I have watched "Judge Judy" on television and she routinely casts vituperations at those who come before her because they, while proclaiming their innocence in some criminal matter, did not fight to the bitter end. She often will opine that she would never give up in court for even the most minor of situations if she felt she was innocent. Judge Judy must be tone deaf or totally ignorant of the lives of most people.

All of us are immersed in our daily activities, challenges and commitments. Any sort of interaction with the police and the law is a dreaded and fearful affair. For many even having an officer stop our vehicle to tell us that a tail light is not working brings about a cascade of psychological and physiological reactions that in part mimic panic and the fight or flight response seen in many animals. We know at such times that the officer has total control over us and can say or do anything. And most of the time even the most minor of offenses results in some sort of citation whether deserved or not. Rarely, very rarely will any court take the word of a citizen over that of a police officer. The burden of proof falls squarely on the citizen to demonstrate his innocence.

All of us have also received justified citations. We fuss and fume, but are polite to the officer, thank him or her for their efforts, pay the fine and get on with our lives. I only know of one person who has never been stopped by an officer. Donnas is about 65 years old, has had a vehicle all her life and has never received a ticket for anything.

But occasionally an officer is having a bad day, makes a mistake or flagrantly issues citations to meet non written quotas from his department. Many municipalities around the country help to finance their yearly budget with revenues secured by law enforcement. And every officer knows implicitly that he has total power over you. Perhaps at one time or another many of us have felt such a situation occurred. And while Judge Judy would say that she would fight to the end to have justice in such a situation, the practical matter of running our lives is usually more demanding than going to court.

By paying the fine on such a citation we plead guilty because the pragmatic value of doing so far outweighs the hassle and cost of trying to fight the injustice. All we want to do is put the trauma of getting a ticket behind us and forget about the occurrence. I, myself, have gotten my share of such tickets over the years. No such situation had been more than for minor offenses. My last ticket was about ten years ago and I did manage to have the citation reduced from a moving violation to a lesser charge. I then paid the ticket.

The consequences of these minor tickets are usually pretty small. Other than paying a fine and having a record of misdemeanors and possibly a rise in our insurance premiums not much else happens. Even more serious situations, like being drunk or possessing drugs, usually only result in a fine.

So while my situation was "only" a misdemeanor with a fine of fifty dollars, the important part for me was more than a belief in my innocence. The State was trying to stop me from engaging in the major activity of my life. Proving that I had a right to my actions was vitally important. And despite my thoughts that Judge Judy did not have the faintest clue as to what most citizens faced when presented with a false citation, in my case I agreed with her and was determined to never give up no matter what.

In a strange way I could devote unlimited amounts of time to my case because of my physical limitations. I had been recovering from my back operation when I discovered that I needed two new hips. And while the operations and hospital stays were only a few days for each, my recoveries took years. I utilized this time to study about the law and for my presenting my defense.

To try when your arms are too weary
To reach the unreachable star

THE GREENBRIER RIVER

The second trial, the jury trial, ended at the beginning of January, 2007. And while the Magistrate, Doshia Webb, decided to postpone the sentencing phase, no date was set. It should be noted that I had already received a sentence consisting of a fine of 50 dollars. By law I could not receive a harsher sentence. If the courts could at their whim make sentences much tougher following appeals then this would have the chilling effect of depriving defendants of their rights to appeal for fear of retaliation. So while having a second sentencing hearing by law was necessary, it was only a formality since the results would have to be the same as before.

Winter is usually a period of storms, blizzards and high water on the Greenbrier River.

Again, my only access to the farm was through the river. Crossing the river even during low water was hard on my vehicles, but the winter added more challenges.

Here in West Virginia temperatures can plunge to -20 F and snows can accumulate to three feet. I could not always just jump into a vehicle and drive away along some snow plowed road. The drive from the log cabin to the river was ¾ of a mile. So for me to even think about going anywhere when there might be a foot or more of snow, meant that I had to plow this driveway. But even if I had done this and even if I could drive through the river I still had a quarter of a mile of access road on the other side to navigate before I reached a hard top road. This, too, could be covered with snow. While my access road was owned by the State of West Virginia it was never plowed and there were no assurances that the hard top road beyond would be plowed. Therefore, trying to get across the river following a snowfall, just to go to the courthouse, could be futile and even impossible.

In addition when the temperature was below freezing, crossing the river, while technically possibly also, introduced another hazard. Driving through the river drenched my brake system and often put water in my transmission, front end and rear end differential. If I stopped for too long at any point after crossing I would be faced with not only my brakes locking up by being frozen solid to the drums or disks, but the gears in any of the drive chain could also be frozen tight.

In winter when the river is "low" its flow rate slows down. Low air temperatures can quickly put a layer of ice on the surface. With a few days of 20 degree temperatures this ice quickly builds into a thick layer that can reach a foot or more. Needless to say that even when days were sunny and bright, without snow and with the river at low levels it would still be impossible for me to cross because of the ice. And even if the days turned milder the ice would persists sometimes for weeks.

But winter in the Mid-Atlantic States is usually not one continuous cold period. Snows are followed by sunny, mild days or even rainy days. Pocahontas County has the highest average altitude of any county east of the Mississippi River. That means we have steep mountain slopes. Even on cold days a bright sun at these altitudes can penetrate a deep snow. The heat from the sun is trapped below the top layer of the snow and the subsequent melted water uses the surface of the frozen ground to quickly create a torrent of runoff which flows into the river. So even with the river low and not frozen a bright sun on an otherwise cold day can quickly raise the level of the river to non-crossable depths. Rain on the other hand unless heavy will usually be bound up in the snow like water in a sponge. The snow could easily soak up this moisture since it only rains on cloudy days. But of course if the rain is heavy or warm then the snow can melt very quickly bringing about a surge in the river flow. Rain alone on the bare frozen ground of these mountains does not sink into the ground and quickly flows into the river. Even if the ground is not frozen it is usually saturated in the winter so that the same fast-paced runoff occurs.

It should also be noted that a sudden rise in the river level brings about other phenomena. The river picks up debris. This can mean silt, topsoil, leaves, branches, trees and even trash are washed into the river. Much of this "flotsam" is carried downstream and into the Kanawha river, which flows into the Ohio River, then to the Mississippi River and finally into the Gulf of Mexico. But some of this debris is caught by eddies and as the river level subsides is deposited as trash along the Greenbrier River. This can really be destructive when the river overflows its banks. I have a lower meadow which accumulates tires, bottles, logs and all sorts of debris when the river is that high. These eddies form in my driveways where they drop into the river.

I have two driveways into the river, one on each side. It is not unusual for the river to rise 6-10 feet or more into the driveways. The eddy that forms in each driveway slows down the flow rate of the river and almost everything settles out. Days later when the river recedes the degree of this accumulation can be assessed. Often there are several feet of muck. I cannot drive my truck through this barrier. I do have a front end loader that can easily dispose of any accumulation on my side of the river, but if the river is still high or laden with ice then I cannot get to the other side to clear that driveway till river levels are "normal" again.

If ice is thick in the winter and there is a sudden rise in the river the hydraulic forces break up the ice into large chunks. The rise in the river increases the flow rate and the ice moves downstream. Just like other debris this ice will pile up in my driveway. It is not unusual in such circumstances for me to have ten feet by ten feet square slabs of ice one foot thick piled four feet high blocking my exit. And again this also occurs in my driveway on the other side. I am unable to drive to the other side until I can get my equipment over there to clear any barriers. Occasionally a large tree will float downstream and wedge itself into one or the other driveways. For this I need to use my bulldozer to remove it. Starting the bulldozer in sub-freezing or even subzero weather can be very frustrating. The dozer does not have an enclosed cab making the long trip to the river brutal.

The river here is lined with large sycamore trees. I had noticed that one side of the trunk of these trees was usually hollowed out well above the level of the river. It took me a couple of winters to realize that when the ice broke up and rode the higher river levels downstream the blocks of ice gouged out the upstream sides of the trunks of these trees.

The United States Geological Survey (USGS) engages in dozens of activities around the country to gather information and to provide data to businesses and citizens alike. One of their tasks is to monitor the stream flow from all the rivers in the United States. To this end they have installed gauging stations along the rivers which measure both the stream flow rate and the height of the river at each spot. Through telemetry this information is transferred in real time each hour through the USGS website onto the Internet. A gauging station is present on the Greenbrier River just several miles upstream from me at a place called Buckeye.

Over the years I have been able to extrapolate the information from the Buckeye gauging station to my position such that I can accurately know the river flow and depth at my crossing without driving the ¾ mile to the river's edge. Additionally, I have learned to be able to read the depth of the river by looking at natural markers on my riverbank at the point where my driveway enters the river.

As might be expected the lower the river the slower is it flows and the higher the river the faster it flows. This is important because moving water is very, very powerful. One cubic foot of water weighs about 60 pounds. A person can walk through a still body of water one foot deep, but put that water in motion and it can easily knock a person down. A couple of feet of still water can cause a vehicle to float and a couple of feet of moving water can carry a vehicle downstream.

I also quickly learned that the type of engine in a vehicle could be of critical importance. Gasoline engines fire from an electrical ignition system. Older vehicles have a battery connected to a high voltage coil which fires the spark plugs through a distributor. Newer vehicles have a more, tech savvy, electronic ignition system. Older vehicles have a mechanical fuel pump; many newer ones have an electric pump and a fuel injection system. The slightest film of water can create a short circuit and cause failure in any vehicle dependent on an electric system. A fan in front of an engine blows air through the radiator and onto the engine to keep it at proper temperature. Should this fan contact the river or even get splashed with water it can spray water onto the electronic, ignition system causing the vehicle to stall.

Diesel engines on the other hand operate on the high heat of compression generated in the cylinders of the engine to ignite the fuel. Fuel is pumped to the cylinders mechanically. In theory a diesel engine can run under water as long as it can get air to ignite the fuel. Therefore, vehicles propelled by diesel engines are the most suitable for my situation.

Additionally the exhaust system of each engine is important. A vehicle will not run if it cannot get rid of the burnt fumes. Almost all exhaust systems are under the vehicle and would be under water if the river level was up by only a foot or two. In most instances the pressure of these gases will keep the exhaust system clear as long as the vehicle is running when it enters the river. If a gas engine were to stop in the river the entire piping, catalytic converter and muffler system under the frame would fill with water. Under these conditions there might not be enough pressure from the cylinders to push out all the water in order to restart the engine.

On the other hand a diesel vehicle with its high compression engine can blow out that water allowing the vehicle to restart should it stall.

For all these reasons I have purchased pickup trucks with diesel engines and high ground clearance.

Another useful tool was a USGS website called the Early Flood Warning System for Pocahontas County. Rain gauges placed in about 15 locations all around the county recorded and displayed on the Internet the precipitation accumulation at 15 minute intervals. By using this website I could see the amount of rain that had fallen and how much was localized or widespread over the entire county. With this information I could determine with accuracy how much water would flow into the river and how long it would take for the river at my crossing to be affected.

The winter of 2007 seemed to me to be a typical winter. I had lived at Point of View Farm by this time for seven years and had been able to experience a wide range of conditions allowing me to accurately predict the impact of the weather and the river on my being able to cross. All of the above situations with the weather and the river occurred that winter of 2006-2007. Doshia, Tony and I kept in touch as they were eager to have the sentencing hearing, but it was not until February that the weather and the river allowed us to put it on the schedule. For me this lull was great. I spent five weeks taking care of my animals, engaging in easy projects and just enjoying myself. I had not seen another human during this time. What a wonderful period in my life.

It was also during this time that I worked on two other motions to present to Doshia's court just prior to the sentencing. Again, I knew that this would be simply a formality and that she would deny the motions, but I wanted to make sure I did everything I could to overturn the jury's decision.

One motion was titled **"Motion to Vacate, Set Aside the Guilty Verdict or Declare a Mistrial."** In a case whereby the judge or a jury has declared a defendant guilty this decision can be reversed by the judge if she accepts the contentions of the defendant that certain facts had been overlooked or misrepresented by the State.

The second motion was titled simply **"Motion for Judgment of Acquittal."** I felt that exercising all my rights and explaining my position again in these motions would be helpful for my appeal to Circuit Court.

I submitted these motions to the court just before sentencing and Doshia denied them.

Chapter 16

This is my quest
To follow that star
No matter how hopeless
No matter how far

SENTENCING

For me the sentencing hearing seemed like it would be just another formality. We would all meet in the courtroom and Doshia would simply reaffirm the fine of fifty dollars. The night before, however, I was talking with another friend, Michael, who asked me if I was going to present an allocution. Now this fellow lives alone up in the mountains and has no legal background or experience. Revealing my total ignorance, I had to tell him I had never even heard the word. He explained that it is the comment a convicted person can make to the court just before sentencing. You see it happen all the time on TV shows, he explained. The convicted person gets up and tells the court he "did not do it" or "yes, I am so sorry."

Of course I then knew what he was talking about, but I did not know the process had a word. After the conversation I immediately researched the word "allocution."

I discovered that indeed I could present to the court anything I wanted to say. I decided that I would even make it more formal by writing out my statement. I worked most of the night putting what I wanted to say together. As I got further into the wording I realized that I was going to really vent on the State, the prosecutor and the judge. I was going to be very forceful, but I also feared that since I was going to step on Doshia's toes pretty hard, that she might use it as an excuse to find me in contempt of court.

In court that day were my usual group of friends and supporters. I told Doshia that I had an allocution I wanted to read, but she asked Tony if he had anything he wanted to say first. Interestingly, Tony went into a long monolog not only about how guilty he considered me, but how he found it offensive that I called him a liar and scoundrel in court. He went on how he was an officer of the court and bound by protocols which prevented him from personally attacking me. I thought he was going to cry, but I knew it was all theatrics. Indeed he was a scoundrel and a liar.

I had made written copies of my allocution which I then handed out to everyone in the courtroom. I did not want anyone to be confused about what I was saying. When I got to the point where I attacked Tony I looked straight at him and emphasized my comments. This entire process in my mind had been an example of a kangaroo court almost down to the kangaroo. Below is the document I used and from which I read.

IN MAGISTRATE COURT OF POCAHONTAS COUNTY, WEST VIRGINIA

STATE OF WEST VIRGINIA

VS   CASE 05M- 381

JOEL ROSENTHAL

Move for allocution

Thank you, Your Honor,

Respectfully I submit the following remarks, and I would like to emphasize Respectfully,

When I set up Point of View Farm, to be an animal sanctuary I went to great lengths to make sure that my actions in regards to dealing with the wildlife of West Virginia conformed to all the laws right down to dotting the Is and crossing the Ts. West Virginia unlike most other states does not have a formal animal rehabilitation program, but that does not mean the existing laws do not allow for this activity. I therefore contend that with my ruling from the IRS and WV business license that I have not broken any law in WV in regards to the care of the fawn addressed in this case. 20-2-4 is very clear in that one can be authorized to possess wildlife. 61-8-19 is very clear in that it is a crime to abandon any animal in need. 20-2C-1 is very clear in that a license is a permit is a public document. No where in any WV statute is there any further definition of what authorization means. In addition many administrative procedures and even hunting regulations allow for the possession of wildlife in a wide array of concepts.

It is interesting in this particular case that throughout the proceedings many others in authority have either violated the law or bent and distorted the law without even a reprimand. Conservation officers Duffield and Shinnaberry violated my WV and US constitutional rights. Mr. Tatano throughout these hearings has stonewalled the defense, distorted the law and outright lied to the court. At an early hearing he flat out lied when he stated that one needs permits to possess exotic animals. At another hearing he fabricated his proclamation that growing an illegal plant like marijuana was equivalent to possessing wildlife, his written response to the Circuit Court about my motions for dismissal showed a total lack of understanding about the applicable laws, about his understanding of the English language, its construction or even what a definition is. In court he storm trooped his way to introducing prejudicial and highly inflammatory information and engaged in prosecutorial misconduct when he lied directly to the court and the jury. In addition he grandstanded with his motion for mistrial and denied me even the right to tell the jury what officer Duffield said in my closing arguments.

Her honor also deprived me of certain basic rights. The law 29A-5-2 guarantees the defendant the right to vouch the record. By denying me this right Respectively, Your Honor, you broke the law and I doubt if any charges will be brought against you.

In addition, Your Honor, if one simply looks at the facts in this particular incident it is clear that I did not take the fawn from the wild; that the DNR did not acquire the fawn when called by Mr. Stoots, but gave authorization for the fawn to be returned to the wild. For me to aid in that act is consistent with the law. Officer Duffield even testified that there is no illegal possession as long as the fawn has free access to the outside. The picture of the fawn in the front seat of an open truck conforms to this definition and the State introduced no evidence what so ever indicating that I deprived this fawn of its access to the wild.

The burden is on the State to prove that I possessed this fawn illegally and contrary to the statements of its own witness, Duffield. This they have not even come close to doing. They have not introduced one piece of evidence to show that I in any way illegally possessed that fawn. NOT One.

I have to therefore admit to some real consternation in regards to how everyone on the bureaucratic side of this case has conducted themselves. It seems that I have been the only one to have obeyed all the laws of WV while all the rest have either broken the law or at the very least distorted it. As a lay person I am the only one without a title. I do not call myself Esquire, Conservation Officer or Judge. Doesn't it seem strange to all of you that you seem to be protecting your power and your titles rather than the law? I doubt very much if anyone connected with my prosecution will be called to task for their usurpation of the vary statutes all of you swore to protect. Yes, it is very disturbing that those who seek or sit in judgment of me seem to have such little respect for the institution which is at the cornerstone of this state and our Democracy. No doubt many of you have already put another notch on the walnut stock of your respective conviction shotguns, but I, a common citizen, will still seek the justice I deserve.

Finally, I would urge Her Honor to overturn this conviction based on all the facts and render a judgment of NOT GUILTY.

Thank You, Your Honor

Joel Rosenthal
28 February 2007

Well, when I finished Doshia looked like she was going to explode. Here this upstart, Joel Rosenthal, had not only dragged her through the grinding mill for over a year and elongated what she considered an open and closed matter, but now he was attacking everything about the judicial system and foremost the judge. Her response was not long, but tart and to the point.

She told me that she resented my inability to accept responsibility for the crime I had committed and that she only wished she could modify my sentence to make it much harsher. She then reaffirmed my fifty dollar fine and adjourned the court.

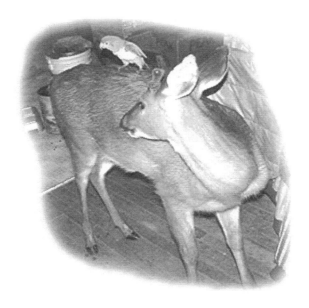

Chapter 17

To fight for the right
Without question or pause

CIRCUIT COURT II

After my first conviction in Magistrate Court, I appealed that decision to the Circuit Court. Circuit court judges are elected officials. In the past they had been noted for making decisions disproportionately in favor of the State. Many such judges had sought to someday be elected to the West Virginia Supreme Court. I had been warned that my case might just be in vain because of this. I was also warned that these judges will if possible take the path of least resistance. That is to say that the judge will spend as little time as possible on any case.

This turned out to be true with my first appeal. Judge Joliffe, who had been the chief circuit court judge, handled my appeal quickly by remanding the case back to the Magistrate Court rather than addressing my many motions for dismissal. While there are about 55 counties in West Virginia, Pocahontas County and Greenbrier County to its south are the largest. Therefore, two judges based in the town of Lewisburg, WV served these counties. The newest judge was Joseph Pomponio Jr. who had been a family court judge before he was appointed by the Governor to fill the vacancy left when Judge Joliffe retired. The other judge was James Rowe who had been serving for many years.

I filed my appeal as before and soon found out that Judge Pomponio would preside over my case. This encouraged me because I felt that coming from family court Judge Pomponio would be conditioned to actually listening to the points being made by the parties and ruling on the applicable law. My hope was that he would not yet be polluted by this convention of thinking the State was always correct.

The court room for the circuit court is on the second floor of the courthouse in Marlinton. This placement is in direct contrast to the magistrate courtroom which is in the basement. Since the circuit court usually hears more serious cases it is large and spacious with fine woodworking throughout. Of course the circuit court also hears cases like mine which are appealed from magistrate court decisions.

Of interest to me in this courtroom was the placement of the "furniture" for the litigants. The judge's chair was elevated about four feet and behind a desk. Assembled ten feet beyond the front of this podium were the many rows of "church pew," bench seats for spectators. And unlike magistrate court in the basement, this room had a high ceiling with metal tiles and ample windows to let in the outside light. But directly in front of the judge, barely a few feet from him, were the desks and chairs for the lawyers and their clients. For me this chair and desk were so close to the judge that I could only see the top of his head. Tony seemed comfortable with the arrangement and sat through all our hearing time, but I had to have a more direct visual contact with the judge. So, just as I did in magistrate court I stood throughout any proceeding in circuit court.

The clerks in the circuit court office established a hearing date and sent me a notice that "Oral Arguments" would be heard on the 7th of June 2007. In attendance, that day, along with me and Tony were a few of my friends and Drew Tanner, the reporter for the Pocahontas Times. Also there was a deputy from the sheriff's department, who served as the bailiff, and a court reporter.

Judge Pomponio immediately noticed that I was standing and thinking I was nervous encouraged me to sit down. I explained to him that I could not see his face from my chair and that I was much more comfortable anyway by standing. He was not used to this and seemed a little uncomfortable himself with my position.

Judge Pomponio asked me about my appeal and as I tried to explain it to him, Tony immediately chimed in interrupting me with a statement about how I thought my business license entitled me to care for wildlife. I began to explain to Judge Pomponio about my West Virginia Business license, about my charitable status with the United States Internal Revenue Service and how it all tied together with the Statues of West Virginia when he simply asked to see the documents. I had supplied him with copies of everything prior to this hearing, but I guess he did not even look at the folder. Fortunately I had more copies with me so I handed them to the circuit court clerk, who then went back to her office to copy them. Without further ado the judge simply announced that he would look at the documents and render a decision.

Eleven days later Judge Pomponio filed with the Circuit Court office his decision. I received a written copy in the mail a couple of days later. The document was five pages long, but I knew that the crucial part would probably be on the last page. I, therefore, turned immediately to the last page.

The fifth page read as follows:

It is, therefore, ORDERED and ADJUDGED that:

1. **The Defendant's business license and the issued Certificate of Authority provide him with the requisite and necessary authority to be considered a "duly authorized agent" to whom Chapter 20, Article 2, Section 4 of the West Virginia Code is explicitly held inapplicable.**

2. **The Judgment of the Magistrate in denying the Defendant's Motion to Dismiss the Charge of Illegal Possession of Wildlife (2) was not in conformance with the law, therefore, the judgment is hereby reversed and the charge against the Defendant for violation of Chapter 20, Article 2, Section 4 of the West Virginia Code is dismissed.**

The Clerk is directed to forward a copy of this Order to the pro se Defendant, Assistant County Prosecutor Tony Tatano, and the Magistrate Court of Pocahontas County.

Entered this the 14th of June, 2007.

Wow, I said to myself over and over again. And of course I reread this last page a dozen times before I read the first four pages. EXONERATED!!!! I could not really believe it. Amazingly, **I HAD WON**. And not only had I won, but I did so in Circuit Court where the decision had much more meaning and clout. This decision not only covered my "possession" of Aspen, but addressed everything I was doing for wildlife. Or at least so I thought. After all, this was West Virginia. But, but, but, surely the DNR had to accept this judge's decision. Isn't that what the courts are for?

That day I called all those who had supported me and, also, informed Drew Tanner, the Pocahontas Times reporter.

It had now been two years since I had been charged. Aspen had grown and was out in the forest. And the irony is that over this time my activities had not changed. Each year I had received more fawns and other animals in need of care. I still had hawks and owls that could not be released under my permanent care. Other migratory birds had over the two years been treated and released as had squirrels, skunks, opossum and other mammals. And despite all the court actions and my two previous convictions, each spring people still brought me more orphan fawns which I raised.

I even remember having a conversation with Walt Weiford where we speculated on how I would have to lose all the lower court decisions before I might be able to petition the West Virginia Supreme Court of Appeals to hear my case. It had all been "tongue in cheek" bantering. Now that course of action seemed impossible since I had just been found innocent.

It is amazing how naïve we as citizens can be when we think that our legal system is JUST. Less than one month later I found myself engaged in the initial process of facing the West Virginia Supreme Court of Appeals.

Chapter 18

To be willing to march into Hell
For a heavenly cause

AMAZING

Now the last time I looked at the Fifth Amendment to the United States Constitution I was sure it protected all of us against double jeopardy. It states: **nor shall any person be subject for the same offence to be twice put in jeopardy of life or limb.** Once a citizen is exonerated in a criminal trial the State cannot revisit the charge and try to convict the person all over again. Even in the most egregious cases this amendment protects those thought to be guilty by the public or even those who later admit to their guilt. The best public example of this was the not guilty verdict O.J. Simpson received from the jury in his trial for murder in California in 1995. O.J. went on to write a book, "If I Did It," where he vividly describes the murders, but because of the

Fifth Amendment he could not be tried again for this crime even though he seemed to admit to committing them.

In 1955 during the racial strife in our country a black boy, Emmett Till, living with his uncle in Mississippi was kidnapped and killed. Two white men were charged with the murder. Both were acquitted by an all-white, male jury. Moments later the men boasted about how they had killed Emmett. Both were protected by our Constitution and never charged again..

More importantly this amendment protects everyone who is truly innocent and receives a "not guilty" verdict against an overzealous prosecutor or State determined to harass an innocent citizen.

Well, I had been exonerated by Judge Pomponio and found not guilty. Judge Pomponio even went so far as to document the error made by Magistrate Doshia Webb in her lower court. My trial was a criminal case. Surely there could be nothing more that the State could do to reactivate my case.

But barely four weeks after receiving Judge Pomponio's ruling and order, I received a long document of 18 pages from the West Virginia Attorneys General's office entitled **"Petition for a Writ of Prohibition."** This was a case filed in the West Virginia Supreme Court of Appeals by Walt Weiford, Pocahontas County's main prosecuting attorney, as the Petitioner against The Honorable Joseph C. Pomponio, Jr. At the bottom of the first page was the name, William Valentino, Assistant Attorney General.

Of course I had never heard of a Petition for a Writ of Prohibition, what it was for or what it could mean. I read the document several times trying to make sense of the content and understand what was being said.

The first thing I noticed was that this document was a legal attack by the State on Judge Pomponio declaring that he did not have the right to rule in my favor. Technically Judge Pomponio was the defendant in this case. Of interest to me was that Walt Weiford was the Petitioner. Now this amazed me because I knew from our conversations that Walt wanted no part of this and never would have drafted this document. The wording was also not in the style of Walt's writing, nor would he take the time necessary to put together such a Petition just to try to convict me again.

Without further procrastination I went to Marlinton to chat with Walt about this Petition. When he confirmed that he had nothing to do with the Petition I challenged him as to how William Valentino could use the Office of the Attorneys General to "forge" his name on this document. Walt tried to explain how "this was the way it is done," but of course I was not satisfied. I challenged him to call up the Attorney

Generals' office and the West Virginia Supreme Court of Appeals to insist that this Petition be nullified and that William Valentino be charged with forgery.

Walt tolerated my visit and verbal gyrations, but he had already been through the grinding mill in regards to my case when he was leaned on by the "higher ups" in Charleston to make sure I was charged and prosecuted.

William Valentino, Esquire had written this document and had clearly used all his legal skills in an attempt to demonstrate that Judge Pomponio had erred in his decision and that the decision should be reversed, leaving the guilty verdict of Doshia's magistrate court.

Well, color me stupid, naïve and an admitted tyro at the law, but I thought that making judicial decisions in criminal cases was exactly what circuit court judges did.

Now it was obvious that Judge Pomponio's decision really struck a nerve in the craw of those bureaucrats in Charleston, WV. Each agency of the West Virginia Government has a lawyer from the Attorneys General's office assigned to it to advise the agency and to represent it in court litigations. William Valentino was the lawyer now assigned to the Department of Natural Resources (DNR). He replaced Kelly Goes, who had appeared in magistrate court to quash my subpoena of Frank Jezioro, the Director of the DNR, prior to my first magistrate trial.

The Petition was complete with a table of contents. One heading was called a "Statement of Facts." Nothing could be farther from the truth. From the "Get Go" I could see that William Valentino, Attorney at Law for the State of West Virginia was a perfect fit for the State, for he did not tell the truth..

When nationwide surveys are done and analysis conducted on the integrity and competence of the legal systems of each state, West Virginia routinely ranks at the bottom.

From the first page of this Petition to the last, William Valentino embodied the art of distortion, fabrication and prevarication.

Now I have to insert at this point that citizens are only required to adhere to the laws as they are written, not as others would like to interpret them. Nowhere in Code 20-2- 4, "The Illegal Possession of Wildlife," does it say that an Authorized Agent to possess wildlife has to be authorized by the Director of the DNR. As a matter of fact my permits from the U.S. Fish and Wildlife Service "Authorize" me to possess wildlife in West Virginia. I do not have, nor do I need a document from the Director of the DNR affirming this.

And nowhere in the decision and order from Judge Pomponio does he say that my business license and IRS status is an authorization from the Director of the DNR. He simply said that these documents authorized me at the State level, not an agency level.

Yes, William Valentino immediately in his "Statement of Facts" presents non-factual information that Judge Pomponio said I was a "Duly Authorized Agent" of the DNR. Valentino repeats this falsehood over and over throughout the document.

At another part Valentino states:

"It may also be said that neither a Certificate of Authority nor a business license may create an implied agency relationship with a governmental agency."

At no time did I ever assert that my authorization was to establish a relationship with any government agency let alone the DNR or its director. The law only states that I have to be authorized to possess wildlife.

Will Valentino continued this false premise where he sought relief in his:

ASSIGNMENT OF ERROR

The Circuit Court exceeded its legitimate Authority when it ruled that a West Virginia Certificate of Authority and a Business License create an agency relationship with the director of the Division of Natural Resources.

Will Valentino then extended his false analogies into a slightly different realm. It is true West Virginia Code 20-2-3 states:

"The ownership of and title to all wild animals, wild birds, both migratory and resident, and all fish, amphibians, and all forms of aquatic life in the State of West Virginia is hereby declared to be in the State, as trustee for the people." Valentino continued by saying **"The Division of Natural Resources has broad authority to regulate the manner in which wildlife may be taken, killed or obtained pursuant to W.VA. Code 20-2-4.**

What Valentino did not understand was that "broad authority" is not "exclusive authority."

Chapter 20 of the West Virginia Code is devoted to Natural Resources. It is in this chapter that the Director of the DNR obtains his power. But it is also in this chapter that his power is limited. Chapter 20-2C-1 explicitly acknowledges the powers of the Governor in regards to wildlife. And then Chapter 20-2C-1h states:

"License" means any license, permit or other public document which conveys to the person to whom it was issued the privilege of pursuing, possessing or taking

any wildlife regulated by statute, rule, regulation or ordinance of a participating state.

Nothing could be clearer as to the authorization given to me by the State in regards to my business license, the validity of that license and my authorization by the U.S. Internal Revenue, a federal public document.

Will Valentino did acknowledge in his Petition that he could not directly appeal the decision of Judge Pomponio because it was a criminal case, but he nevertheless thought it appropriate to obfuscate the law and to engage in an end around, flanking movement to achieve his goals. All I could think was how much Frank Jezioro, the Director of the DNR, must have hated me.

In his Petition Will Valentino moved the West Virginia Supreme Court of Appeals for an immediate hearing and the issuance of this Writ of Prohibition.

Within two weeks I filed the following long response to the Clerk of the West Virginia Supreme Court of Appeals:

In the West Virginia Supreme Court of Appeals
Charleston, West Virginia

STATE EX REL., WALTER W. WEIFORD PROSECUTING ATTORNEY POCAHONTAS COUNY, WEST VIRGINIA
PETITIONER,

V,

THE HONORABLE JOSEPH C. POMPONIO, JR., CIRCUIT JUDGE OF THE 11TH JUDICAL CIRCUIT,
RESPONDANT

RESPONSE TO PETITION FOR WRIT OF PROHIBITION, FILED BY WILLIAM R. VALENTINO, ASSISTANT ATTORNEY GENERAL

NOW COMES JOEL ROSENTHAL, A PARTY TO THE ACTION

In order for a writ of prohibition to be valid it must meet either of the following standards.

PROHIBITION, WRIT OF - The name of a writ issued by a superior court, directed to the judge and parties of a suit in an inferior court, commanding them to cease from the prosecution of the same, upon a suggestion that the cause originally, or some collateral matter arising therein, does not belong to that jurisdiction, but to the cognizance of some other court.

The writ of prohibition may also be issued when, having jurisdiction, the court has attempted to proceed by rules differing from those which ought to be observed or when, by the exercise of its jurisdiction, the inferior court would defeat a legal right.

Clearly the first standard does not apply since the case has already been heard and adjudicated. No current writ can be used to address this issue.

In an attempt to adhere to the second paragraph Mr. Valentino would have to demonstrate that the Honorable Judge Joseph C. Pomponio proceeded by rules differing from those which ought to be observed or that he exceeded his jurisdiction.

Mr. Valentino clearly does not understand the law or the statute 20-2-4 because unlike just about any other statute in West Virginia this one specifically states that actions of wildlife possession are legal when "duly authorized." In addition there is no requirement for anyone so authorized to be an agent of the Director of the DNR, but simply an agent of the State. An Agent of the Director would be a Conservation Officer, an employee or an administrator. Citizens are not "agents of the Director unless so decreed by the Director or members of his agency"

Further the Governor also has the power to authorize the possession of wildlife WV Code 20-2C-1h which states:

§20-2C-1. **Governor's authority to execute.**

ARTICLE I. FINDINGS AND DECLARATION OF POLICY AND PURPOSE.

(h) "License" means any license, permit or other public document which conveys to the person to whom it was issued the privilege of pursuing, possessing or taking any wildlife regulated by statute, rule, regulation or ordinance of a participating state.

Here any license, permit or public document allowing for possession of wildlife is sufficient for "authorization." By Mr. Valentino's logic since I am authorized by this statute I would be an "agent of the Governor."

Since NO WHERE in the West Virginia code is the term "duly authorized" defined, Judge Pomponio proceeded and applied **correctly** all the rules and to the letter all the applicable laws that would normally be at his disposal. Since any land owner can be authorized to possess wildlife without an individual permit or license, then for sure the West Virginia Secretary of State can make such an individual determination. **In addition Judge Pomponio recognized that because of these rules and laws his order on this matter was within the bounds of all judicial proceedings and jurisdictions. Nor in any way was he legislating from the bench, but simply applying the existing laws.**

At no time did I, Joel Rosenthal, assert that with my business license was I an agent of the Director or acting on behalf of the Director. And at no time did Judge Pomponio assert that I with my business license was an agent of the Director, just an "agent" of the State.

Now interestingly, testimony from Mr. Harvey, a witness for the state, revealed that indeed the WV DNR authorized without specification that this particular fawn be returned to the wild. **By assisting in this endeavor I would have also been an authorized agent of the Director and in compliance with 20-2-4 according to Mr. Valentino.**

Judge Pomponio's judicial sphere is the applicable laws and all their words. At no time did he exceed this authority.

None of Mr. Valentino's court cases arise from a statute specifically allowing for the activity in litigation, nor are they criminal in nature. Thus his "examples" are irrelevant and immaterial.

Mr. Joe Manchin, II, therefore, also, exercised his position correctly and accurately when he issued his Certificate of Authority and declared that my application for a business license "conforms to law." Judge Pomponio recognized this and ruled appropriately.

That Mr. Valentino and Mr. Jezioro, Director of the DNR do not like the wording of the laws is regrettable, but their remedy if any should be directed at the legislature, not the Supreme Court. It should also be noted that all the statutes in Chapter 20 were drawn with the aid and consent of the WV DNR. The Legislature did not construct 20-2-4 in a vacuum. Mr. Jezioro is obligated to recognize this and should, therefore, not attempt to scapegoat Judge Pomponio for following the law, but at his own organization for its role in helping to formulate the statute.

It is also very clear that in the absence of being able to file an appeal in this case, Mr. Valentino **thinly veils his document as a Writ when in reality it is an appeal or certiorari.**

IN THE SUPREME COURT OF APPEALS OF WEST VIRGINIA
September 2006 Term No. 33175

STATE OF WEST VIRGINIA EX REL. THOMAS TAYLOR, MELODY AND DARYL JOHNSON, AND LEONARD AND IRIS LUCAS,

Petitioners

v.

THE HONORABLE DAVID W. NIBERT, JUDGE OF THE CIRCUIT COURT OF ROANE COUNTY, NATIONWIDE MUTUAL INSURANCE COMPANY, AND GEORGE G. O'DELL, JR., AND STACY MCKOWN O'DELL

Respondents

SYLLABUS BY THE COURT

1. **"Prohibition lies only to restrain inferior courts from proceeding in causes over which they have no jurisdiction, or, in which, having jurisdiction, they are exceeding their legitimate powers and may not be used as a substitute for [a petition for appeal] or certiorari."** Syllabus Point 1, *Crawford v. Taylor*, 138 W.Va. 207, 75 S.E.2d 370 (1953).

Surely, Mr. Valentino cannot pull the wool over everyone's eyes. His document is an appeal disguised as a "Writ of Prohibition"

Mr. Valentino and Mr. Jezioro clearly think they have a dispute with the wording of the law in which case they have petitioned the wrong body of our government. Let them seek whatever remedy they wish in the legislature.

For all these reasons this "Writ of Prohibition" has zero merit and deserves no further attention by your Honors, Justices of the Supreme Court.

However, because Mr. Valentino submitted to the court a document 28 total pages in length I feel that it is appropriate for me to address all his allegations. I should note that from beginning to end his document contains many errors of fact, omissions, distortions, fabrications and attempted manipulations. All of this presents a credibility gap that puts into question his entire position and its motive. It is also clear to any impartial observer that Mr. Valentino employs the age old tactic of throwing garbage against a wall, hoping something will stick.

A perfect example of this is his "exhibit 2, pages 1-7" at the back of his document. Here he presents H.B. 4125 which was introduced to address a mechanism for animal rehabilitation. On the surface one might think that the State of WV has a formal mechanism so that orphaned and injured animals can be helped. **What Mr. Valentino does not tell you is that the DNR lobbied ferociously to kill this bill and was successful.** They claimed among other things that the DNR did not have the funds to implement such a program. Yet, somehow the DNR was able to assist Three Rivers Avian Center, a private migratory bird center, with a substantial monetary donation for the construction of a bird facility. The DNR cares not one lick about helping individual wildlife and actually goes out of its way to kill any such animals.

Ironically, Mr. Valentino acknowledges that H.B. 4125 is not law at the bottom of page 9 in very small print. This begs the question as to why he included in his Writ this House Bill in the first place. Was it just diversionary to make Your Honors think that there were other mechanisms for animal rehabilitation?

Another example of Mr. Valentino's disingenuous position can be garnished by the **absence of any examples of damage or injury to either the DNR or the State of West Virginia by my activities.** Mr. Valentino presents no court cases of injury or damage, no testimony, no expert witness and no documentation to support this contention. Mr. Valentino seems to be simply endorsing the current policy whereby all injured or orphaned animals are either allowed to die or killed by conservation officers. Mr. Valentino, thereby, wants the Justices to believe on his word that if I aid any animal the State is somehow injured. **None of us should make the mistake to think that their document is about injury or damages to the State, nor about the law, or even about helping animals. The only "injury" seems to be to Mr. Jezioro's ego and that is not an actionable injury.**

Almost every other state finds benefit from those who aid their wildlife. Mr. Valentino has no credibility when he proffers that the DNR's current policy, which is the inhumane treatment of wildlife, somehow benefits the State. Mr. Valentino also does not address WV Code 61-8-19 which states:

§61-8-19. Cruelty to animals; penalties; exclusions.

a. **If any person cruelly mistreats, abandons or withholds proper sustenance, including food, water, shelter or medical treatment, necessary to sustain**

normal health and fitness or to end suffering or abandons any animal to die,... he is guilty of crime.

Under this statute I would have been guilty of cruelty to animals had I abandoned this fawn. And indeed every time a DNR officer maltreats an animal he/she too should be charged as a criminal. In effect the DNR wants to place citizens in a catch 22 situation whereby they are deemed a criminal if they help wildlife and a criminal if they abandon wildlife.

The West Virginia Supreme Court recognized that statutes in *pari materia* should be construed together:

Supreme Court of Appeals of West Virginia.
William F. JULIAN
v.
Frank DeVINCENT et al.
No. 13043.
Submitted Sept. 14, 1971.
Decided Nov. 2, 1971.
Dissenting Opinion Nov. 8, 1971.

Under this doctrine I cannot be placed into a catch 22 situation whereby no matter what my actions I or any other citizen would be guilty of one statute or the other.

Again for all of the above examples Mr. Valentino and the DNR have no valid position. They obfuscate and distort the facts creating a vacuum of credibility and for these reasons alone and combined with the above should have their "Writ" (Appeal) dismissed outright.

Likewise Mr. Valentino's "Statement of Facts" (page3) contains important errors of omission. Mr. Valentino conveniently left out (on page 4 second paragraph) the fact that Mr. Harvey, a witness for the state, **testified that he had contacted the DNR prior to bringing the fawn to me and was authorized to return the fawn to the wild.** Fearing for the fawn's safety he brought it to me so that I could aid in this endeavor giving the fawn a greater chance for survival. **This I did. My actions simply conformed to what the DNR authorized. Ironically, this means that for this particular incident and for this case I was indeed an authorized agent of the Director.** This fact alone should have exonerated me in the eyes of the Magistrate. Again this omission by Mr. Valentino short-circuits his credibility and willingness to tell the entire truth. He does not want you to know that I acted legally and responsibly throughout.

Also on page 4 at the bottom and onto the next page, Mr. Valentino fails to give you all the pertinent facts. Not only did I obtain that "Scientific Collection Permit" after further discussion with Ms. Sargent but I have also had "game farm" permits to raise and release pheasant and quail. And of course Mr. Valentino, in addition, fails to mention that I have several migratory bird permits from the US Fish and Wildlife Service. These permits comply with all the laws of West Virginia as delineated in Chapter 20-2-4 and require no input or further authorization from the WV DNR, nor do they make me an agent of the Director.

Believing anything put forth by Mr. Valentino from a legal, moral, or factual basis for me is very difficult. I present this not only to refute Mr. Valentino, but also to point out that all of this is really more irrelevant and immaterial fodder being thrown by Mr. Valentino against the wall hoping something will stick.

Mr. Valentino again with his "Assignment of Error" attempts to throw more dirt at that wall. His proclamation (bottom of page 5) that Judge Pomponio exceeded his authority is a perfect example of his use of arrogance in an attempt to ramrod his point of view through your court. Just look at how he uses a larger, bold, all cap type. The reality is that Judge Pomponio read the law (20-2-4) and understood that the words allow for the possession of wildlife when duly authorized. He then looked for any definition of what duly authorized was and could find none. Again there is no contention by the Judge or by me that I am via my business license an agent of the Director. Mr. Valentino clearly thinks that if he slams this concept at Your Honors enough times you will believe him.

Thus Mr. Manchin was perfectly within his authority to issue that business license to me and Point of View Farm, Inc. See attached exhibit). All of this is consistent with the law and all the words of the law (20-2-4). My activities are not illegal.

Mr. Manchin would never have issued someone a business license to say, grow marihuana, or to print money, but had anyone asserted that he did, Judge Pomponio would have recognized the ruse and upheld the conviction. But had another judge in this situation ruled that printing money was legal Mr. Valentino would have legal grounds for his Writ of Prohibition because there would have been no underlying statute that would make these activities legal. In this case against me there is an underlying statute authorizing the activity thus making moot Mr. Valentino's contention.

Again if he and the Director do not like the law they should take their beef to the legislature not the Supreme Court. And once again I would like to point out that **none of Mr. Valentino's examples of case law supporting his "Writ" have at their core a criminal statute that allows for the activity in question.** Therefore the Writs approved in those cases are irrelevant to this case. Mr. Valentino tries again and again to sidestep this issue and it is critical. Judge Pomponio has full jurisdiction to apply the law (20-2-4) as it is written to this case.

Throughout his "Standard of Review" Mr. Valentino over and over tries to tell the court why he has the right to file his Writ of Prohibition (appeal), but that, too, is not the point. Because Judge Pomponio acted appropriately **your Honors do not have to even hear Mr. Valentino's pleas. They are ill founded and not appropriate.**

On page 7 Mr. Valentino lists what he calls "grounds for issuance of a writ of prohibition." This he gleaned from

SUPREME COURT OF APPEALS OF WEST VIRGINIA
September 2001 Term FILED RELEASED December 13, 2001 No. 29103 December 14, 2001
STATE OF WEST VIRGINIA EX REL. KEVIN CALLAHAN, Petitioner Below, Appellant
v.
HONORABLE KATHERINE SANTUCCI, MAGISTRATE, Respondent Below, Appellee

But what Mr. Valentino does not tell you is that the court wrote the following:

3. "A writ of mandamus will not issue unless three elements coexist—(1) a clear legal right in the petitioner to the relief sought; (2) a legal duty on the part of respondent to do the thing which the petitioner seeks to compel; and (3) the absence of another adequate remedy." Syl. pt. 2, State ex rel. Kucera v. City of Wheeling, 153 W. Va. 538, 170 S.E.2d 367 (1969).

It is clear that Mr. Valentino cannot meet any of these three conditions. And again for this reason Your Honors should not even consider his "Writ."

Likewise throughout his "Memorandum of Law" page 8 Mr. Valentino misses the point again. **Of course I and Point of View Farm, Inc. have to follow the law and that is exactly what I have done.** Mr. Valentino's focus on corporations, foreign corporations and nonprofit corporations is a red herring calculated to divert your attention from (again) the wording of the law (20-2-4). There is nothing in this law that makes a distinction between individuals or corporations, foreign or otherwise.

On page 9 he again diverts your attention to the ownership of animals. I have never claimed that I own any wildlife in West Virginia, but only that I am the caretaker for some. As an example Mr. Valentino fails to acknowledge again that 20-2-4 yields to the migratory bird act. I currently have an owl, two vultures, and a red-tail hawk. All of these birds are within my care via the US Fish and Wildlife Service and have nothing to do with the State of West Virginia. And again they do not make me an agent of the Director. Since it is the State that claims ownership the DNR's roll is to only administer to certain aspects of this ownership. The DNR only acts as a fiduciary in that ownership.

Another example of wildlife possession in West Virginia without any document of permission occurs when a land owner can "hunt" many species year round without making any contact or obtaining any written permission from the State or the DNR. And none of these animals need be killed since there is no requirement that hunting leads to killing.

See current rules and regulations for hunting page 2 bottom, page 6 and page 8 and

WV code 20-1-2 Definitions:

"Hunt" means to pursue, chase, catch or take any wild birds or wild animals: *Provided,* That the definition of "hunt" does not include an officially sanctioned and properly licensed field trial, water race or wild hunt as long as that field trial is not a shoot-to-retrieve field trial.

"Take" means to hunt, shoot, pursue, lure, kill, destroy, catch, capture, keep in captivity, gig, spear, trap, ensnare, wound or injure any wildlife, or attempt to do so: *Provided,* That the definition of "take" does not include an officially sanctioned and properly licensed field trial, water race or wild hunt as long as that field trial is not a shoot-to-retrieve field trial.

One can see from this definition that hunting does not automatically mean killing. So a farmer who wanted to raise a woodchuck could do so without any contact, paperwork or interference from the state or the DNR by simply "hunting" and capturing a baby woodchuck. He does not have to kill it and since the season is open year round he can keep it forever. It is in the law and in so doing no such farmer has to seek or receive an agency relationship with the Director.

Likewise would Mr. Valentino argue that a mounted deer's head on someone's wall belongs to the State or to the hunter? And I wonder to what ownership Mr. Valentino would ascribe the bass on a fisherman's dinner plate? So once again he presents to you half-truths and fabrications. This process of distortion continues when he again tries to tie me into some sort of agent for the Director. I do not claim to be such for purposes of my business license, nor does Judge Pomponio's ruling. And nowhere is there any link in the law that says possession has to be or not be a form of rehabilitation. Mr. Valentino's attempt to make this link is ludicrous. End of paragraph 3 page 9.

It is of interest to note that on page 10 paragraphs 3 and 4 of his Writ (appeal) Mr. Valentino confirms that the state has no mechanism for a formal appeal, but throughout this document he has played a salesman's game of bait and switch with me, Judge Pomponio, .Walt Weiford and all of you Justices. This document of his is really an appeal disguised as a Writ of Prohibition. For this reason, too, it is hoped that Your Honors will refuse to hear his plea.

At the bottom of his page 10 Mr. Valentino cries about damages. It is impossible for anyone to contemplate how acts of kindness, concern and aid put forth by a person with decades of wildlife experience can be considered damaging to the DNR or the State of West Virginia. Mr. Valentino fails to address this point with any facts, cases, testimony or words of substance. Again it is requested that the court reject this "Writ" (appeal) on this hollow claim of damage.

I do want to thank Mr. Valentino for stating (top of page 11) and publishing last page (Exhibit 3) my E mail to Captain Pizzino. This correspondence confirms that my intentions and activities are to aid our wildlife and with Judge Pomponio's ruling I do so legally. Until or unless there is a stay or reversal of this decision Mr. Valentino's comment that my actions are criminal is a form of harassment and intimidation. He has no standing to proffer this opinion and I object to his self-serving and erroneous comment.

On Pages 11, 12 and 13 Mr. Valentino again hackneys his same errors of law of Director relationships and of his misguided attempt to overturn Judge Pomponio's decision and calling me a criminal.

I have included (for those who did not receive his cc) a letter sent to me by Mr. William Valentino dated 2 July, 2007 and my response to his letter.

Request for Relief

I, Joel Rosenthal, obey all the laws and statutes of West Virginia, right down to the very last letter.

I, Joel Rosenthal, also request relief from this malicious pursuit of me. For over 2 years I have had to face a plethora of court dates in order to obtain a valid ruling from Judge Pomponio. Over this time I have had to overcome the vast resources and power of the State of West Virginia.

Judge Pomponio made his ruling on the written words of the law. This falls within his judicial jurisdiction. **He did not legislate from the bench**. His authority to make this decision is clear and well established. WV Code 20-2-4 is clear in that it provides a mechanism for the legal possession of wildlife via authorization. No matter what he does Mr. Valentino cannot erase these words from the statute.

Throughout my response to Mr. Valentino's "Writ" I have addressed and refuted every one of his allegations and claims

Mr. Valentino and Mr. Jezioro clearly do not like the wording of the appropriate laws, but that does not mean they should seek relief with the West Virginia Supreme Court. They obviously were absent the day each branch of our government was discussed in their high school civics class.

Throughout his document Mr. Valentino ponders how he and the DNR might seek a law more defined along their own prejudicial lines. Hopefully, Your Honors will direct them from your chambers to the appropriate legislative body down the hall without hearing their appeal (writ).

I, Joel Rosenthal, reserve the right to edit this filing to correct any error and/or to add supplemental material.

Respectively submitted:

Joel Rosenthal _____ July 2007

CERTIFICATE OF SERVICE

I, Joel Rosenthal, defendant in the lower Circuit Court do hereby affirm under penalty of perjury that I have given copies of this document to the:

Clerk of the West Virginia Supreme Court
Room E 317
1900 Kanawha blvd., Bldg E
Charleston, WV 25305
Via registered mail _____July, 2007

Joel Rosenthal _____July, 2007
Honorable Joseph C. Pomponio, Jr.
Circuit Court, 11th Judicial Circuit
200 North Court Street
Lewisburg, WV 24901

Via registered mail _____July, 2007
Joel Rosenthal _____July, 2007
Mr. William R. Valentino
Assistant Attorney General
Capitol Complex, Bldg 3
Room 669
1900 Kanawha Blvd, East
Charleston, WV 25305
Via registered mail _____July, 2007
Joel Rosenthal _____July, 2007
Walter Weiford

Prosecuting Attorney
Pocahontas County
Marlinton, WV
In person _____July, 2007
Joel Rosenthal _____July, 2007

To my amazement the West Virginia Supreme Court of Appeals on September 13, 2007 without a preliminary hearing granted Valentino's petition in a vote of 3-2.

See announcement below:

| 4. | William R. Valentino (Counsel for the Petitioner) Pro Se (Respondent) Pocahontas - Pomponio Grant 3-2 Davis and Starcher | Petitioner in **State ex rel. Walter W. Weiford v. The Honorable Joseph C. Pomponia, Jr., No. 072193**, is the prosecuting attorney of Pocahontas County who seeks a writ of prohibition to prohibit the circuit court from enforcing an order dismissing criminal charges against Joel Rosenthal. |

Chapter 19

And I know if I'll only be true
To this glorious quest

WEST VIRGINIA SUPREME COURT OF APPEALS

Most states use an intermediate appellate court to handle the appeals from Circuit Court such that their Supreme Court is not overly burdened with cases. While the West Virginia Constitution allows for an intermediate appellate court, the state has chosen to allow cases to go directly from the Circuit Court to the West Virginia Supreme Court of Appeals. Because of this the West Virginia Supreme Court of Appeals hears more cases than just about any supreme court in the nation. The new upcoming session for the court was scheduled to begin on the 8th of January, 2008.

Five Justices comprise the Court in West Virginia. They are all elected for 12 year terms. Each rotates into the Chief Justice position. Brent Benjamin, Larry Starcher, Spike Maynard, Joseph Albright and Robin Davis (the only woman) were the Justices considering my fate.

In cases involving a Petition for a Writ of Prohibition against the decision of a Circuit Court Judge the court usually rendered a decision devoid of a hearing, but would allow the grieved party to present its side if it chose to do so at a scheduled hearing before the Court in Charleston, WV, the State Capitol. The actual defendant in these cases, The Circuit Court judge, ironically did not participate. It was therefore up to the lawyer (in this case me) for the affected entity to defend the Circuit Court judge's decision. So while the direct litigants in this case were the State of West Virginia and Judge Joseph Pomponio, the Supreme Court following its vote granting the Petition on September 13, 2007 sent me a ruling by the Court:

"commanding and directing the said respondent (Joel Rosenthal) to show cause if any he can, why a writ of prohibition not be awarded against the Honorable Joseph C. Pomponio, Jr., a Judge of the Circuit of Pocahontas County, as prayed for by the petitioner in his said petition."

At this point I was psyched. At least I would now have the chance to present my case directly to these Justices. But, but, but, I thought to myself I should not forget that my role was to defend Judge Pomponio and his decision. I had to make sure that I knew the law and did not wander off onto a tangent about how I liked animals or how wonderful they were.

It was obvious to me that the Justices had not read my response to Valentino's Petition, but I knew that I had to continue sending them material as I saw fit. It might just be important for them to have everything on record. Besides they could "accidentally" pick up my documents and read them. And in my mind it might just be possible for them to reverse their decision prior to our Hearing. They still had a few months before the 2008 session of the court convened. So with diligence I put together a Brief complete with references to court cases.

By asking around I was told that a Hearing before the Justices adhered to a strict protocol. Mr. Valentino would have the opportunity to present his position, I would then be able to refute his contention that Judge Pomponio had erred and then Valentino would have a final say. Throughout, the Justices might and would interrupt each of us to pepper us with their own questions or statements. I was told that I would have about 10 minutes to present a "prepared statement."

For a couple of weeks prior to our Hearing I practiced and practiced my "prepared statement."

I had lived at Point of View Farm for almost eight years by the beginning of 2008. Never in all that time, had I felt I absolutely had to cross the river. There had been a few handfuls of situations when I had appointments or wanted to cross the river, but could not because it was too deep or because of ice. On each of these occasions I simply postponed my trips. Going to the Supreme Court in Charleston would be different. I had to make sure that I got to Charleston that day.

For a week or so before the Hearing I kept an eagle eye on the weather and the river. The temperatures were not too cold and no rain or snow was in the forecast. The river was even free of ice. For added insurance two days before the Hearing I took one of my trucks across the river and parked it at a neighbor's house so that even if I had to swim or canoe across the river I would have a vehicle to drive to Charleston.

Chapter 20

That my heart will lie peaceful and calm
When I'm laid to my rest

THE HEARING

Years earlier I had met a woman, D.L. Hamilton at a neighbor's house across the river from my farm. D.L. it turns out is D.L. Hamilton, Esq. who works as an Assistant Attorney General in the West Virginia Attorneys General's office in Charleston. She also lives one block from the Supreme Court.

I had not consulted D.L. or even discussed my case with her, but she was a friend. Not knowing about traffic and parking at the Capitol Complex in Charleston I decided to contact her to see if I could park at her house the morning of the hearing. She not only consented, but gave me directions and invited me to come early for coffee.

Charleston is a three hour drive from the Farm. The Hearing was scheduled for 10 AM so I wanted to make sure I not only got there on time, but left myself lots of margin in case of any mechanical difficulties. The morning was clear and cool.

I decided by design that I did not want to dress to "look" like I was trying to be a lawyer. I did put on a nice pair of slacks, a patterned shirt and a camel hair sport coat. I wore NO tie. I wanted the Justices to see and feel that I ran a wildlife animal sanctuary and that all I wanted to do was help the animals of West Virginia. The Justices, prior to sending me the notice to appear, had already voted against me and Judge Pomponio so while Will Valentino would be the "schooled" spiffy Attorney General lawyer, I had to show I knew the law. I also had to be a "psychologist" who made the Justices like me and what I did. After all this was not a life or death case, there were not millions of judgment dollars on the line. I wanted them to embrace the Bambi concept.

Almost every kid has seen the Walt Disney animation film of Bambi, the white-tail, deer fawn whose mother is killed by hunters. And in real life fawns are considered by most along with bear cubs to be loveable and cuddly. With soft spotted brown hair and large brown eyes fawns are almost irresistible. I knew I had to play on this image.

Several of my friends who had attended all the other proceedings said they were going to be there as did Drew Tanner, the reporter. John Leyzorek met me in Hillsboro at 6 AM so that we could ride together. On the way I practiced my "speech."

The trip went fine and as we relaxed at D.L's home she asked me about how I intended to approach the Court. I told her about my ten minute "presentation."

Well, she did not exactly break into a wild laugh, but she did inform me in no uncertain terms that I would not be given a ten minute presentation. Not only that, she said, but the Justices would be interrupting me, making statements and asking me questions as I tried to talk. The entire process could be over in 10 to 15 minutes, she said.

Like Will Valentino, D.L. had been before the Supreme Court presenting cases on behalf of the State. And while she took more casually the outcomes, having won some and lost some, she recognized that my demeanor was anything but casual. If I knew my material I should just try to be relaxed and at ease, she advised.

I told her that from the information I got from the Court that I had been scheduled for a 10 AM Hearing. Everyone, she offered, received the same time, but in reality my case would be heard in the order it was on the docket.

D.L. made a call to the court and then told me which case came before mine and that both might not be heard till after the lunch break.

I decided to be at the Court by 10 AM anyway so that I could become acquainted with the appearance and demeanor of the Justices, how they responded to different lawyers and just how the entire process unfolded.

John and I walked to the courthouse, found the courtroom and signed in. The room held a couple of hundred people and just about every space was filled.

The courtroom was brought to order and draped in their long, black robes the Justices entered. Cases were called and heard. None were criminal cases. To me they were all boring civil cases. At no time were any decisions rendered and in my mind it was impossible to see if one side or the other had an advantage.

I thought from the order of the cases that mine had the chance of being heard in the morning, but this was not to be. Looking around I found my supporters. At the lunch break we all chatted. Several cases were still ahead of me so it would be mid-afternoon before I would have my hearing.

John and I went outside at the break to catch some fresh air and saw D.L. coming towards the courthouse. I offered to take the three of us to lunch and D.L. suggested a restaurant nearby.

Back in the courtroom that afternoon, John and I moved to the front row of the seats as my Hearing approached. We were the only ones this close.

I have noticed this many times at public events. People just seem not to like to sit in the front row. I guess we feel that we then become conspicuous and the focus of attention.

So there we were in the front row of the Supreme Court right in front of the Justices. Not only could I tell they saw us, but they took careful note of us. I doubt if they had seen a "mountain man" like John before. And I knew they were looking at John's boots. Of course at this point they did not know who we were or why I was there or which of us was the "defendant."

In front of the Justices and just to each side of them was a small desk for the representatives of each side. Protocol again places the State to the right facing the Justices and the other party to the left.

My case was called and I went to my desk with a pencil and a folder containing some paper. I wanted to be able to scribble notes if necessary.

And the world will be better for this
That one man, scorned and covered with scars
Still strove with his last ounce of courage
To reach the unreachable star

"YOU ARE VERY ARTICULATE AND A GOOD LAWYER"

Will Valentino presented the State's case by repeating his same lies about my being an agent of the Director of the DNR. Judge Pomponio never said this. Valentino went on to say that the case was one of the" rule of law and that even though it was a criminal case that I, once the exoneration was overturned, could file my own appeal to the Supreme Court. He even had the audacity to say," You have to have respect for the law." Valentino then went on to equate what I do to help animals with people who break the law by engaging in assisted suicide. Chief Justice Maynard saw through that ruse and jumped all over Valentino. After Maynard suggested that I rendered pretty good care for this "creature," Valentino went off on another tangent and somehow made a reference to people who shoot dogs in the head to kill them.

Judge Maynard then hit Valentino with a basic concept of the law by saying that since I had a license from the State and believed that what I was doing was lawful, I could not be guilty of any criminal intent.

Judge Albright then tried to support Valentino by saying that it seemed Judge Pomponio just wanted to see "Bambi" grow up and, therefore, he used my business license to make me an agent of the Director.

This persistence by the justices to link me with being an agent of the Director of the DNR just demonstrated to me that none of the Justices read my "Response" and "Brief" to Valentino's Petition.

Justice Maynard then went on to suggest that courts sometimes have a hard time distinguishing between what is right and what is justice.

Valentino was dismissed for the time being and I was given the floor. Since DL Hamilton had convinced me that a "speech" would never do I knew I just had to "wing it." So, I tried to put forth as much information as possible before being asked questions.

I decided to come out firing and to attack even the legality of Valentino's Petition and of the Supreme Court's decision to "grant" it and to even hold a Hearing on the matter. I reminded the Justices that my case was a criminal case and not a civil matter, that I was protected from double jeopardy not only by the U.S. Constitution, but also by the West Virginia Constitution and by West Virginia code. I also pointed out that they had already ruled in another case, WV v Judge Nibert, that in a criminal case a Petition for a Writ of Prohibition could not be substituted for an appeal..

I then informed them in no uncertain terms that Judge Pomponio's decision at no time referenced any relationship between me and the Director of the DNR or the DNR itself. I reinforced this concept by declaring that there were many mechanisms in the statutes by which one could become authorized to possess wildlife and most of them had nothing to do with the Director.

I continued attacking Valentino by pointing out that the statute under which I was charged recognized the role of the Federal Government to license me to possess wildlife and that recognition was devoid of any relationship with the WV DNR or its Director.

Judge Maynard then focused in on the fawn I received. We established that it had been rescued from a lake, that its mother was gone and that it was then brought to me. He then inquired as to what would normally happen to such an animal.

I jumped on that question and with relish described how the DNR routinely violated the Cruelty to Animals Statute 61-8-19 by abandoning animals it knew would perish. Maynard then threw me a curve ball which instead of hitting for a home run, I simply tapped into a grounder.

He asked if the fawn had been abandoned by its mother should the doe be prosecuted. I responded by saying that people could have run the mother away and chased the fawn into the lake, thus absolving the "mother" of any liability.

I followed this with a long monolog describing how I did not go looking for animals in need and that the DNR officers not only knew what I was doing, but had visited my facility. I explained how even the magistrate who convicted me had given me animals when she was a conservation officer for the DNR.

Judge Maynard then went on to suggest that feeding deer was illegal. He described how he had once been given a hard time for doing just that. I forcefully reassured him that feeding deer was not illegal.

After telling the Court again that there are many mechanisms for authorizing someone to take care of animals, I was thrown another curve ball by Judge Maynard. He asked by what mechanism I felt I was authorized and if it was on the basis of my business license. I would like to think that I artfully dodged a direct answer by saying that I was confident in Judge Pomponio's decision and that Judge Pomponio listened to the facts of the case, read the law and applied the law. After all this was supposed to be about Judge Pomponio's decision.

Any tension which might have then been evident was immediately dispelled when His Honor, Chief Justice Maynard exclaimed that he realized that two of the Justices had voted for me when considering Valentino's Petition, but that he could not figure out why he had voted against me. I immediately began laughing along with the entire gallery of spectators.

Up till this point I had suspected that I had done a pretty good job of impeaching Valentino and of supporting myself and Judge Pomponio, but with Judge Maynard's statement I knew that I had won.

At this point I was even more relaxed than I probably should have been because I told him that he voted against me because he wanted to meet me and have me present my case.

Justice Davis then quipped that she voted against the Petition because she "wanted to set me free." This, too, brought laughter, which was further enhanced when Justice Albright remarked that he had only voted against me because the Chief Justice had done so. This brought a comment from Maynard that he wished Albright would vote that way all the time. And this brought more laughter.

Then the Honorable, Chief Justice Spike Maynard paid me the ultimate compliment by saying, **"Mr. Rosenthal you are very articulate and a good lawyer."**

I was then asked to sum up my position. I reasserted the concept that Judge Pomponio acted legally and responsibly, that I did not break any laws and that even if one suspected that a statute was violated there was no clear evidence to the fact. I quoted from the WV Code the definition of the word "License" in regards to the possession of wildlife and how it applied to my case. I then yielded to the Justices by declaring that they knew better than I that when there is any ambiguity in the law the Courts are obligated to find in favor of a criminal defendant.

Justice Davis then let loose with a long explanation of how much important work and time the Supreme Court had to spend on meaningful cases of child abuse and the like and that she questioned the wisdom of Valentino to bring forth such a trivial, petty matter where I was hurting no one.

Valentino was given an opportunity for his final rebuttal. He tried to answer Justice Davis by explaining "why we prosecute traffic violations." This only demonstrated that he did not understand that someone who goes through a stop sign puts the lives of other citizens at risk. My actions threatened no one. Valentino went on to cry about how he had been a defense attorney and a prosecutor and that he was used to having people hate him. But he then lied about how all the issues I had raised had been dealt with in the lower courts.

Justice Albright asked Valentino if he agreed that had I been given animals by officers of the DNR then I would be an agent of the DNR? Maynard went on to suggest that on this basis, the case would be one of *Selective Prosecution*.

Of my many motions to the courts for dismissal *Selective Prosecution* had been one of them.

Maynard then described how nit picking he found the DNR in regards to enforcing all rules. He described how he once had to prosecute a fisherman who had one too many fish, costing the man to forfeit $3,000 worth of fishing gear. "It comes back to the difference between doing the right thing and justice," he said, "THIS OLD MAN IS DOING THE RIGHT THING" referring to me.

And just like that the Hearing was over. It had lasted just about 20 minutes.

There was no doubt in my mind and in the mind of all the spectators that none of these Justices liked the DNR. And there was no doubt in my mind that in front of dozens of his Esquire colleagues, Will Valentino had not only embarrassed himself, but had been embarrassed by me and the Justices. In mountain parlance "he had been taken to the woodshed."

Will Valentino turned from his desk and walked briskly through the center aisle to the door at the rear of the room. I followed closely behind wanting to see if he would shake my hand. I called his name when we reached the door. He turned and I extended my hand. He refused to respond in kind. As he disappeared into the room across the hall I simply said, "Thanks, Will, anytime you want to do this again just let me know."

The Justices had recognized at the beginning of the hearing that this was a case not just about a fawn, but about Bambi. Valentino had begun digging his own grave when he equated my saving Bambi to assisted suicide and had deepened the hole with references to killing dogs by shooting them. When he touted his credentials of having been a defense lawyer and prosecutor in an attempt to diminish my pro se position, his "shoveled hole" deepened. The Justices then buried him by unleashing their disdain for the DNR and the pettiness of this case.

While my overall approach to this Hearing had been a bit tenuous, I certainly was testing the waters as I went along. I definitely learned a valuable lesson about how important psychology was in this interaction.

In a way the Justices were like an established pack of wolves. Both Will Valentino and I were outsider pups who wanted to gain access to the pack and be accepted. Valentino's approach was to be assertive, demanding and pushy. I chose to be knowledgeable, but complementary. Almost from the beginning this wolf pack attacked Valentino, but reached out to me in an embracing manner.

Outside the building I gathered with some of my supporters. D.L. showed up. She had listened to the Hearing which was broadcast on the Internet. She, too, thought I did a fine job. The Justices would arrive at a final decision in about a week. We all surmised a positive outcome.

The three hour ride back to Point of View Farm was delightful as John and I critiqued just about every statement made during the hearing.

Unbeknownst to me, though, there was another surprise from that afternoon. Drew Tanner, the reporter for the Pocahontas Times, after the Hearing, visited a friend of his who ran the National Public Radio (NPR) station in Charleston. Together on the radio they told the story of my case complete with sound bites from the hearing. Later, I was able to obtain and listen to a copy of the broadcast much to my enjoyment.

Three days later on the 11th of January, 2008 the Court entered their order into the records. It read:

On this day came the Court, on its own motion, having considered the petition for a writ of prohibition, the responses, and the oral argument of the parties, and does hereby dismiss this case as improvidently granted.

Judge Pomponio and I had won. The justices had decided that they had been mistaken to have granted the Petition in the first place.

The Circuit Court's decision remained and stood bold to the proposition that I was authorized to possess wildlife in West Virginia. This concept had been affirmed by the highest court in West Virginia.

Or so I thought.

Chapter 22

I am I, Don Quixote,
the Lord of La Mancha
Destroyer of Evil am I

CEASE AND DESIST

For about 2 ½ years the State of West Virginia through its law enforcement and legal system reinforced the notion in me that it was a two-bit, third world, banana republic. Over and over the judicial systems refused to honor and follow not only its own statutes, its own Constitution, but the Constitution of the United States. It also became evident that the legislatures could not write laws that specifically outlined the powers of the department heads. The Department of Natural Resources was a Gestapo organization with a despot as its Director. With unwavering persistence this was proven to me again and again. Before his own court during my hearing, the Chief Justice of the West Virginia Supreme Court of Appeals told of his own experience as a prosecutor when he revealed how he was "forced" by the DNR to charge and convict a man for having one too many fishes in his creel.

One would think that on its surface the Department would have as its mandate and goal the protection and conservation of the State's natural resources. Unfortunately the opposite is true. The Department is hardly more than a for-profit business which brings revenue into the coffers of the State by killing animals and fostering the consumption of the resources. Under the "leadership" of the DNR West Virginia's forests are clear cut, streams are destroyed, whole mountains are removed and dumped into valleys, a pervasive labyrinth of mine tunnels leaches toxic metals into the environment and thousands of citizens are poisoned by simply trying to breathe contaminated air.

One would think that at the grass roots level each Conservation Officer would harbor concern over the welfare of each and every individual animal. And most citizens think that every biologist hired by the department is trained to help any orphaned or injured animal. But, alas, this is not the case. These men and a very few women almost to the very last person without hesitation will neglect, abandon and even shoot wildlife for the flimsiest of reasons. Of course calling any of them a "Conservation" Officer is equivalent to calling Fidel Castro a freedom fighter. It is all propaganda.

The men who rescued the fawn brought to me were told when they called the DNR to simply throw the baby back into the woods to die. In my own county Howard Shinaberry, who had been an officer for over 20 years shot a fawn right in the middle of a community simply because the fawn was hanging around people.

Another officer who saw a dog playing tag with a fawn in the municipality of Lewisburg trespassed onto private property and in front of the family shot the fawn. Frank Jezioro, the director of the DNR responded to the many complaints by the community by casually brushing away the outrage and supporting the officer.

At the very time I was being charged Patti Hoffman, who was a respected animal rehabilitator in the northern part of West Virginia, was about to release 60 raccoons she had rescued. The WV DNR illegally entered her property and with true "Storm Trooper" tactics killed every animal and arrested her.

Just above Marlinton not that far from me a mother bear sow was killed on the road. She had two young cubs with her. The DNR biologist who responded knew about me and could easily have caught or tranquilized these cubs and brought them to me, but chose to shoot them instead.

Without oversight and without requirements to document their slaughter these officers not only kill any animal they want, but also keep their hunting friends happy by issuing "permits" for them to kill deer and bears throughout the summer, ostensibly to protect livestock and fields of corn. Yes, some agricultural damage does occur, but the State reimburses farmers for losses. It is almost impossible to know which bear or deer ate a few ears of corn. Killing them with a pack of hunters and dogs only satisfies the lust in these men.

I know of another situation where a family who had found some orphaned, baby opossum called the DNR, thinking the agency would care for the babies. The officer who responded took out a plastic bag in front of the family and suffocated the babies.

Even more recently, an elk who had escaped from a game farm in Pennsylvania made its way a few miles south and ended up on a person's farm in northern West Virginia. When the DNR showed up all they wanted to do was kill the elk. The farmer, resisted, neighbors were called and quickly the story entered the news cycle. The DNR, eager for blood, sought a court order allowing the destruction of this elk. A public uproar ensued to protect this animal. Finally, the Governor was forced to intervene and give the elk a stay of execution.

But when the West Virginia legislature tries to pass a bill to establish an animal rehabilitation program the DNR puts out a position paper denouncing the bill as too burdensome on their officers. To them killing animals is the easiest manner of dealing with wildlife.

For two weeks following the decision of the Supreme Court to uphold Judge Pomponio's decision I actually forgot that I lived in a state with such disregard for the laws and for any decision the courts might render in favor of a citizen.

I had overcome having several of my U.S. Constitutional Amendments violated, had dealt with a magistrate and assistant prosecutor who violated their oaths of office at every turn and found myself impeaching an assistant Attorneys General lawyer who committed perjury to the highest court in the state. I could not imagine the bureaucrats desiring another food fight with me. I was such a little guy in the full scheme of the State's activities. I lived in the wilderness, away from the maddening crowds. I only helped animals and rubbed elbows with few other humans.

But on the 25th of January, 2008 Frank Jezioro, Director of the West Virginia Department of Natural Resources put his "John Hancock" on a letter addressed to me with a large, bold, font heading entitled

CEASE AND DESIST ORDER

When the certified mail envelop arrived bearing the return address logo of the DNR I have to admit I was very perplexed. But what Frank Jezioro could not understand was that by this time I was having fun. Flushed with success and an aberrant sense of legal knowledge I read Jezioro's letter with a mixture of joy and an inflated feeling of power.

The letter is worth repeating here.

Dear Mr. Rosenthal:

It has come to my attention that you have made public representations of your intent to provide care and/or rehabilitation to wildlife at your Point of View Farm an activity which is currently in violation of the West Virginia Code. Ownership and care of native wildlife is vested with the State of West Virginia, Department of Commerce, Division of Natural Resources.

By the authority granted in me in W. Va. Code 20-1-1, et. seq., I am ordering you to <u>cease and desist</u> all unlawful activity involving native wildlife. Pursuant to the Code, this cease and desist order may be enforced in any court for coercive, remedial, or preventive relief by injunction, mandamus or other appropriate proceedings.

Signed by Frank Jezioro, Director

I read this letter over and over again and chuckled more each time. Of course it was not written by Jezioro, but by "my buddy" William Valentino. Jezioro would not even know the meaning of half the words.

The Director of the WV DNR is an appointed official. He, and the director postion has always been a "he," needs to possess no particular skills. Frank Jezioro seems to have gotten his position because he loved to kill animals. He has dogs which he uses for upland birding and for killing bears.

So I thought to myself both these guys still wanted to rumble. Well, I would just demonstrate that citizens have an entire palette of rights and mechanisms with which to respond to bureaucrats who try to throw around their weight. My confidence was sky high and even though I would still be entering uncharted legal proceedings, I was going to meet their challenge with language and proclamations stronger and more forceful than their own.

If one reads this letter from Jezioro closely, one has to wonder if Will Valentino ever really went to law school, let alone graduated and became an attorney. He opens by declaring that my "representations" of my activities are illegal. Never in the history of the United States can one's "representations" be a focus of a cease and desist order. And for Valentino and Jezioro to make a blanket statement ordering me to stop engaging in any "illegal activity" is absurd beyond description. He goes on to say that "Enforcement of this "order" might include "coercive… relief" and "appropriate proceedings."

Given Jezioro's propensity for using firearms and for manipulating, distorting and rewording the laws, I envisioned him conducting a raid on my property in the same manner he did to Patti Hoffman. Except in my case his officers would open fire, kill me and concoct a story about self-defense. What did he mean by "coercive relief?" While paranoid on its surface this thought of mine not only had roots in past activities of the DNR, but reflected what other people had expressed to me about what the DNR might try to do. Many told me that the DNR would try to kill me.

More importantly I learned that I had gotten to all of them psychologically and that the more they dealt with me the more mistakes they made. A hackneyed cliché states that the best defense is a strong offense. Like a cat playing with a mouse I had the upper hand and was going to make use of my advantage.

My letter responding to Jezioro's contained the following:

As you know Mr. Jezioro an "Order" requires you to inform me specifically of the information you have that any of my current activities are in violation of any WV code. This you have not done. You cannot legally send such a letter to me about some potential future action, nor about some action completed in the past.

And as you know Mr. Jezioro you are also required when you send me such an "order" to inform me of my right to a hearing or an appeal of this matter and by what time limit I have to demand such a right. This you have not done.

And Mr. Jezioro you are also required to file a copy of any such order in the 11th Circuit Court, Pocahontas County, since this is where you allege such violations may occur. This you have not done.

Of course you know all of this from your knowledge of the law and of WV Code 32A-2-22, WV Code 32B-2-10, WV Code 32B-2-11 and WV Code 21-5-15.

So Mr. Jezioro with this letter I am informing you that:

I demand you immediately; send to me any specific information you claim to have which describes any of my current actions as being illegal.

I demand that you schedule a hearing on this matter in the 11th Circuit Court in which jurisdiction you allege I might at some point in the future engage in illegal activities.

I will be filing in the 11th Circuit Court a Petition for a Hearing, a Petition for a Review and or a Petition for an Appeal on this matter.

By this letter I am ordering you, Mr. Frank Jezioro, Director of the West Virginia Division of Natural Resources to Cease and Desist in your publishing or presenting orally any statements about me or my activities which are false, inflammatory, libelous, slanderous, defamatory or which can be construed as damaging my character and good name.

I am demanding that you apologize to me in writing and that you also submit this apology to the media, i.e. the Pocahontas Times and WV Public Broadcasting.

Failure on your part to rehabilitate my good name might result in civil litigation against you, your agency and anyone else that had a hand in assaulting me this way, i.e. Mr. William Valentino.

I am sending this to you via Fax and E mail today the 4th of February 2008, with an original hard copy to follow via certified mail when I am able to cross the river. I should also inform you that you ignore this correspondence at your own legal jeopardy.

It was no surprise that I did not hear back from him. But I had another card to play.

Theoretical astronomers speculate on there being parallel universes. In the West Virginia DNR there truly are parallel universes and I was going to turn up the pressure in the other one, too.

Chapter 23

I will march to the sound of the trumpets of glory
Forever to conquer or die

SCIENTIFIC COLLECTION PERMITS

The possession of wildlife does not simply entail possessing live animals. In the eyes of the WV DNR possession implies having any animal dead or alive or any animal product or by product. Feathers, shells, bones, claws, teeth are but a few of the items included in wildlife possession. Elementary school kids who may collect these items on a field trip are in violation without a Scientific Collection Permit from the DNR. And any citizen who may find and keep such items would be in violation.

Permits, though, may be obtained by approved organizations that included scientific entities and non- profit charities.

When I first arrived in West Virginia I applied for and obtained such a permit to possess dead animal and animal products. Each year I filed a report specifying the items I had collected.

In West Virginia a fellow, Roy Moose, goes around the state doing wonderful informative shows for schools and organizations with the many snakes he has gathered. These were live, sometimes deadly reptiles.

Wondering how he could "legally" possess such wildlife I called Barbara Sargent who managed the Scientific Collection program for Curtis Taylor, Chief of Wildlife Resources, and requested a copy of his application and permit. The permit clearly allowed Mr. Moose to collect, keep, display and release live, wild animals.

Since my own permit was up for renewal I filled out the form using the exact same words as those used by Roy Moose. I had already been qualified to have these permits so making this exact change should not be anything out of the ordinary and it would have in addition to my legal successes given me direct authorization by the DNR.

Well, it was no surprise that my application was rejected. A letter informed me that I could renew my current permit, but not the modified one. This was discrimination in the most blatant form. No reason was given, just the denial. Further correspondence on my part to correct this inequity was unsuccessful so I eventually filed a legal action called a Petition for a Writ of Mandamus in the Circuit Court in Charleston. This was a document designed to have the court force the agency to issue me the permit I requested.

The final status of this Petition remained in doubt for about a year, but this was my way of attacking the DNR in a parallel universe.

Chapter 24

Hear me heathens and wizard and serpents of sin
All your dastardly doings are past

APPLYING THE PRESSURE

For the previous several years I had been the defendant not just from a criminal justice standpoint, but a psychological one. The State and the courts dictated all the activities. Criminal charges were filed; I had to respond. The courts set the hearing and trial dates, I had to attend. And while I "fought" back with my many motions, subpoenas and witnesses I was always the one responding. The "ball" always seemed to be in someone else's hands. The "flow" was being dictated by everyone else.

I believe I handled all of this pressure quite well since in reality I was still a rookie and just trying to learn the law the best I could. There was no doubt that I gleaned encouragement from my friends, the press coverage I had and of course from my success in the courts. Articles appeared regularly in the Pocahontas Times and in the

West Virginia Record, a publication in Charleston. The Record called me the best lawyer in West Virginia.

Now, though, I would dictate the pace. The ball would be in my hands and my new goal would be that of a gad fly that would bite and irritate them into making more mistakes. To me it was perfectly obvious that both William Valentino and Frank Jezioro were already feeling the pressure of losing to this little, old, grey haired, West Virginia, mountain, hillbilly, novice, hick. Valentino would be the first to feel my ire. His total distortion of the facts in his Petition for a Writ of Prohibition and his out-right elementary and parochial lack of knowledge concerning his "Cease and Desist" order, clearly illustrated to me his incompetence.

The saying that it is hard to see the forest when amongst the trees applied. I wondered if all his Esquire colleagues also saw his short comings. And how in the world did he land that job in the Attorneys General's office? His statement before the Supreme Court bragging that he had been a prosecutor and a defense attorney only highlighted his insecurity. Or maybe he was just trying to reassure his fellow lawyers in the court room that he really was an attorney and not just someone dragged in off the streets.

My first order of business was to file ethics charges against him for his prevarications and distortions. The ethics board is supposed to be an independent entity and an activity away from government. And indeed more attorneys in West Virginia are found guilty of ethics violations and indiscretions than just about in any other state. But I knew that the board might just consider him incompetent not ethically immoral. Nevertheless, regardless of what would happen here I would be sending a strong message to him that his fate might now be in my hands, not his own. Besides this action would put him on the defensive, a place I had been for so long.

Following up on this kind of action I contacted the Attorney General, Darrell McGraw and his second in command, Frances Hughes, to tell them of Will Valentino's indiscretions and legal incompetence.

A secondary goal of mine was to make contact with any and all bureaucrats who had associations with Will Valentino and Frank Jezioro. By leaning on these other people I was putting pressure on everyone such that they, too, would become irritated at my tactics and do what they could to end this fiasco.

The Division of Natural Resources is part of the Department of Commerce. Interestingly, the new Secretary of Commerce was now Kelly Goes, the same lawyer who I forced to come to Marlinton in 2005 to answer my subpoena to Captain Pizzino. She was now the boss of the DNR Director, Frank Jezioro, and I let her know of his violations of the law.

All major employees in the West Virginia government have e-mail addresses. So rather than send formal letters to both Valentino and Jezioro and the others, I chose to "keep in touch" with them via the Internet. And with such correspondence I would not use their titles or last names, only their first names as a way of knocking them off their imperial pedestals and bringing them down to my earthy level. I was going to keep them informed of my thoughts in a very informal, in your face, sort of way.

My friend, John Leyzorek, thought these tactics were somewhat belittling of me and might diminish my position and clout, but I argued that these men had over and over considered me to be beneath them and had tried to intimidate me. The "Cease and Desist" letter was just the latest. Besides I now knew that they were "worried" about me because they tried to use the law to retaliate against me. I had pricked their hides and they could not stand it. This fervor by them to keep swatting at me as though I was an infected mosquito only demonstrated their own vulnerabilities. I knew that just by buzzing around their ears I could elicit a wild, frenzied response.

More so, though, they had committed this egregious act with their "Order." I responded with demands of my own which carried legal implications. They ignored apologizing to me at their own peril.

So as a follow up to my response, I e-mailed Jezioro that I had taken care of an animal and that if he believed this act was illegal he was obligated to come and arrest me. I told him I welcomed any attempt he might make to support his "order" so that we could see what would happen. And I told him that if he did not arrest me then he was either condoning my activity or he was a conspirator to the crime he said I was committing. Like the coward he was, he did not arrest me, nor did he respond.

I wrote Valentino and told him that I had just learned that his wife was an attorney and I was wondering how he felt to be the second best lawyer in his own family.

Another long Email to Jezioro went as follows:

Frank,

This morning I was listening to a very motivational song and found myself singing along with my voice growing louder and louder. It was a song about standing up to tyranny. Of course I immediately thought of my own struggle with you and the State of West Virginia over my right to help abandoned and needy wildlife. Of course one of the most interesting aspects of how we each have approached this

situation is that I stand for principle while you stand for power. I don't believe you have a cell in your body that cares one bit about the wildlife of West Virginia. To you our wildlife is nothing more than a commodity, a resource to be mined like coal and timber. All you care about are the revenues wildlife can create, and the power you can wield from your office. How tragic that now one day many who graduate from our high schools when asked about their academic areas of interest will say they graduated with a degree in hunting. How dare you demean our citizens with such an intrusion into their studies. There are many reasons that West Virginia is last in just about any measure of the quality of life for our citizens. You and your policies contribute largely to this degradation.

Your willingness to violate your oath of office, to continue to attempt to intimidate me even after the courts have ruled what I do is legal is a testament to the evil extremes you will entertain in order to try to assert your abuse of power.

Well, Frank I welcome your challenges because my stand for principle will always be in your face of tyranny. And long after you are back in your insurance office I will be helping any animal brought to me. The difference is that I will gain comfort from knowing that my efforts simply to do what I can are rewarding enough. You though will now go through the rest of you life knowing that I will always be in your mind as someone who put decency ahead of your Gestapo tactics.

It is truly tragic that West Virginia is so full of men like yourself. Maybe one day we will regain the ability of our citizens to stand on our own two feet and not subjugate ourselves to those who would exploit us and our resources.

Currently I am re-reading a book I have in my library. It is called "All I Really Need to Know I Learned in Kindergarten," by Robert Fulghum. Frank, I strongly recommend this book to you and to all your staff. And if there are any concepts in it that elude you feel free to contact me or any 5th grader in Charleston.

So bring it on Frank. In the long run you do not stand a chance because you are evil. I have mentioned to you before that my middle name is David. I can therefore assure you that I carry in my sling enough stones to slay as many Goliaths like yourself as is necessary.

Calls are beginning to come to me more frequently about animals in need of care. Given that your agency has NO mechanism for assisting these animals and returning them to the wild I am honored that I can help fill that void for the entire great state of West Virginia.

Maybe one day we will have a DNR director who will recognize the contributions folks like me can provide to our entire state.

I also want to take this opportunity to remind you that we have a court date here in Pocahontas County on the 4th of April. I have subpoenaed you to be my witness against yourself. What a wonderful opportunity. And of course I will finally have the chance to attach your face to your name. I hope you, too, will enjoy our gathering as much as I will.

Joel Rosenthal

Point of View Farm, Inc.

My barrage of E mails to both Jezioro and Valentino continued until I decided to file actions against them.

Judge Pomponio had told me in court that he would hear any cases I might file in Circuit Court. I appreciated this, but I also knew that actions against WV Government officials were supposed to be filed in the Kanawha County Circuit Court since that was where the state capital, Charleston, was located. But I also knew that another lawyer from the Attorneys General's office would have to come all the way from Charleston again to object to my filing actions in the Circuit Court in Pocahontas County.

One of my filings was the Petition for a Writ of Mandamus against the DNR for refusing to issue me my valid, yet modified, Scientific Collection Permit. The other filing was a law suit against Will Valentino, Frank Jezioro, Mike Pizzino, the captain of my DNR district and the two DNR officers in Pocahontas County who had violated my Constitutional rights.Once a preliminary hearing date had been set I also subpoenaed Frank Jezioro. Sure enough Tom Smith, Managing Deputy Attorney General, arrived early and presented the judge with a prepared Order dismissing my case and one to quash my subpoena for the Director of the DNR. At the hearing, Smith also reminded Judge Pomponio that my filings in the Circuit Court in Pocahontas violated the venue statute outlining the Rules of Procedure..

My response was that I knew the protocol had been for me to have filed in Kanawha County, but that, he, Judge Pomponio, had told me he would hear any civil suits I brought.

Smith wanted both my cases dismissed forcing me to re-file or drop the Petition for a Writ of Mandamus and the lawsuit. But all of us, including Judge Pomponio knew the law and that a judge could simply transfer the cases to the other Circuit Court. This he did.

While I was leery of this guy, Tom Smith, he and I did engage in some beneficial conversation. He had come to court with his college age son so I invited them to visit Point of View Farm to see what I did. They agreed to follow me back to the river so I could transport them across.

The visit was delightful. They enjoyed my place and the animals. I could tell that he seemed more on "my" side" than the Defendants.

I was now on my way to learning about civil law. By this time I had spent several years being my own criminal lawyer. Now it was time for me to get the hang of civil law.

I had patterned the format for my cases from those I found in the circuit court files and from the Internet. Little did I know, though, of the manner in which the wheels of justice turn when cases are filed against government officials or employees.

My Petition for a Writ of Mandamus was pretty straight forward. It simply requested the court to reverse the prejudice demonstrated against me by the DNR. I provided all the documentation I thought was necessary.

My law suit on the other hand was pointedly focused on how I had been violated by these officials. Below is a copy of my filing.

Plaintiff- Joel Rosenthal   **Case Number:**

Defendant- Frank Jezioro,
 Director of the West Virginia Division
 Of Natural Resources (WV DNR), Charleston, WV.
 Mike Pizzino, Capt in the WV DNR, Elkins, WV,
 Howard Shinaberry, WV DNR Conservation Officer, Pocahontas County
 Shane Duffield, WV DNR Conservation Officer, Pocahontas County
 William Valentino, Esq. Attorney General's Office, Charleston WV

Type of Case: Misc. Civil, Defamation. Libel, slander, violation of Civil and Constitutional rights

---

Jury Demanded Yes

Filed by:

Joel Rosenthal, pro se

_____   _____

Signature   **date**

SUMMONS

 In the Circuit Court of Pocahontas County, West Virginia

Joel Rosenthal, Plaintiff

V   Civil Action No._____

Frank Jezioro, Defendant

IN THE NAME OF THE STATE OF WEST VIRGINIA, you are hereby summoned and required to serve upon Joel Rosenthal, pro se Plaintiff, whose address is HC 64 Box 136A, Hillsboro _____

Clerk of the Court

CIRCUIT COURT OF POCAHONTAS COUNTY, WEST VIRGINIA

Joel Rosenthal,
Plaintiff

Civil Action No._____

Frank Jezioro,
Director of the West Virginia
Division of Natural Resources,
Defendant
Mike Pizzino, Capt WV DNR
Howard Shinaberry, Conservation Officer WV DNR
Sean Duffield, Conservation Officer WV DNR
William Valentino, Attorney, WV Attorney General's Office

COMPLAINT

Now comes the plaintiff, Joel Rosenthal, pro se by way of Complaint against the Defendants and State as follows:

1. The plaintiff, Joel Rosenthal, is a citizen and resident of Pocahontas County, West Virginia.

2. The plaintiff, Joel Rosenthal is president and runs Point of View Farm, Inc., a non-profit charitable organization established as an animal sanctuary in 2000 in Pocahontas County, West Virginia.

3. Point of View Farm, Inc. became a 501, (C) (3) non-profit organization with the IRS on the 5th of October, 2000

4. Point of View Farm, Inc. obtained its business license to operate in West Virginia on August 20, 2001 for the "care and preservation of abandoned and needy wildlife."

5. On Sunday, May 29th 2005 the Plaintiff, Joel Rosenthal received an orphan deer fawn.

6. On or about Tuesday 31 June, 2005 Capt. Mike Pizzino of the WV DNR met with Conservation Officer Howard Shinaberry in Elkins WV, informed him of an allegation that the plaintiff might have a new born fawn and ordered Shinaberry to violate the Plaintiff's US and WV Constitutional rights and Civil Rights and to drive directly to Point of View Farm and without obtaining a Search Warrant to enter said property and search.

7. Conservation officer Howard Shinaberry of the WV DNR had been to the above property in the past by invitation and was aware of the No Trespassing signs at the head of the driveway.

8. On or about the 31st of June, 2005 Capt. Mike Pizzino thus violated his oath of office to obey the Constitutions of the United States and of West Virginia by failing to inform Officer Shinaberry of his obligations to obtain a Search Warrant to enter the property known as Point of View Farm, Inc.

9. On or about Tuesday, 31, June 2005 Howard Shinaberry violate the Plaintiff's US and WV Constitutional and Civil rights by driving directly from Elkins, WV to Point of View Farm in Pocahontas County where he violated 5 NO TRESPASSING signs and searched said property without even the presence of the Plaintiff. Shinaberry found nothing and confiscated nothing.

10. On or about 31 June, 2005 Officer Shinaberry did violate his oath of office to obey all the laws, rules and regulations of West Virginia, its Constitution and of the US Constitution by entering the posted No Trespassing property known as Point of View Farm, Inc to conduct an illegal search.

11. On or about 3:45 Pm on Wednesday 1 June 2005 Officer Shane Duffield Conservation officer of the WV DNR in Pocahontas County without a Search Warrant violated 5 NO TRESPASSING signs at the head of the driveway to Point of View Farm and drove ½ mile where he was met by the Plaintiff in front of a barn.

12. When challenged to produce a Search Warrant Defendant Duffield became indignant, agitated and hostile toward the Plaintiff and admitted that he had no Search Warrant.

13. On or about Wednesday 1 June, 2005 Officer Duffield did, thus, violate his oath of office to obey all the laws, rules and regulations of West Virginia, its Constitution and of the US Constitution by entering the posted " No Trespassing" property known as Point of View Farm, Inc to conduct an illegal search.

14. On August 9th 2005 Frank Jezioro through his agent Conservation Officer Shane Duffield filed criminal charges against the Plaintiff for the illegal possession of wildlife.

15. After two trials on this matter in magistrate court in Pocahontas County and after two appeals to circuit court Judge Joseph C. Pomponio, Jr. ruled on 14 June, 2007 that indeed the application and business license of Point of View Farm, Inc. sufficed to authorize the plaintiff to care for the above wildlife in West Virginia.

16. The Defendant, Frank Jezioro, through his attorney, Mr. William Valentino, then threatened the Plaintiff with further prosecution via a letter dated July 2, 2007. This despite the fact that no reversal, appeal, vacation or impeachment of Judge Pomponio's ruling had been rendered. This crass attempt to usurp the law and court rulings through documents which are public are most disturbing and have slandered, defamed and libeled the Plaintiff.

17. As an employee of the State of West Virginia, Defendant William Valentino took an oath of office to obey all the laws, rules and regulations of West Virginia, its Constitution and of the US Constitution

18. The Defendant, William Valentino, garnishes no immunity from his obligation because he is an attorney. As a matter of fact William Valentino is more

obligated to act according to the law and any court ruling because of his position in the Attorney General's office.

19. The Defendant, William Valentino, did violate his oath with his letter of July 2, 2007 informing the Plaintiff that he, Valentino, had no intention of obeying the lawful ruling of Judge Pomponio of the 11th Circuit Court.

20. With this letter of July 2, 2007 the Defendant, Frank Jezioro did violate his oath of office to obey all the laws, rules and regulations of West Virginia, its Constitution and of the US Constitution

21. Still not satisfied the Defendant through Walter Weiford, Pocahontas County prosecuting attorney, and William Valentino, Assistant Attorney General filed a Petition for a Writ of Prohibition against Judge Pomponio with the West Virginia Supreme Court of Appeals.

22. On January 8th 2008 after granting the Petition provisionally the West Virginia Supreme Court of Appeals heard oral arguments from the Plaintiff from the Plaintiff and from William Valentino of the Attorney General's office.

23. On January 11th 2008 the West Virginia Supreme Court of Appeals ruled that It had improvidently ruled in favor of the Petition and was reversing this position by upholding the ruling by Judge Pomponio.

24. Once again not willing to abide by the law and the Court's decision the Defendant, Frank Jezioro, this time under his own signature on 25 January, 2008 sent the Plaintiff a letter titled "Cease and Desist Order" demanding that the Plaintiff refrain from acting in accordance with the rulings of the courts. The Defendant, Frank Jezioro, did, thus, violate his oath of office to obey all the laws, rules and regulations of West Virginia, its Constitution and of the US Constitution. .

25. Again with this correspondence, a public document, the defendant, Frank Jezioro, libeled, slandered and defamed the Plaintiff by accusing him of violating the law despite the Court's decision to the contrary.

26. The Defendant, Frank Jezioro, took an oath of office to defend and obey the Constitution and all the laws, rules and regulations of the State of West Virginia. By threatening the Plaintiff, the Defendant has violated his position and office and engaged in an egregious abuse of power.

27. The Plaintiff as was his right demanded a hearing in Circuit Court to force the Defendant, Frank Jezioro, to justify his "Cease and Desist Order." The Defendant refused to appear for the hearing.

28. The public was further informed of the Defendant, Frank Jezioro's, Cease and Desist Order via an article in the Pocahontas Times.

29. The plaintiff asked the Defendant, Frank Jezioro through E mails to issue an apology and a retraction of his illegal Order. To this date the Defendant has failed to even respond.

30. As a further direct and proximate result of the Defendants' actions the Plaintiff has been defamed, slandered and libeled damaging his reputation at running a non-profit corporation and his personal reputation within the community.

31. As a further direct and proximate result of the Defendants' actions much negative publicity has been disseminated via the print media and the internet about the Plaintiff and Point of View Farm, Inc. inhibiting the Plaintiff from fully engaging in constructive activities for the business.

32. As a further direct and proximate of the actions of the Defendants and The Resultant publicity the Plaintiff has been forced to explain his adherence to the law to those who inquire about his non profit charitable organization. The subsequent diminution of donations to the charity is substantial.

33. In addition to being illegal, negligent, careless, reckless and unwarranted the actions of Defendants were willful and unwarranted and evidenced a criminal indifference to the civil obligations owed to the Plaintiff, therefore entitling the Plaintiff to punitive damages.

WHEREFORE the Plaintiff demands the following relief:

1) That the Defendant, Frank Jezioro, Director of the West Virginia Division of Natural Resources be ordered to issue an immediate apology via a registered letter to the Plaintiff for the Division's and the Defendants' having slandered, defamed and libeled the Plaintiff in documents which by their very nature are public entities with access by all citizens..

2) That the Defendant, Frank Jezioro, Director of the West Virginia Division of Natural Resources be ordered to issue an immediate apology via a registered letter to the Plaintiff for violating the Plaintiff's Constitutional and Civil Rights.

3) That the jury and or court order the Division of Natural Resources, through it director to reimburse the Plaintiff for any and all expenses incurred through this law suit.

4) That the court award as it sees fit any and all punitive damages to the Plaintiff for the egregious and illegal acts of the Defendants, all employees of the West

Virginia Division of Natural Resources or of the Attorney General's office acting on behalf of the WV DNR.

5) That the jury/court award the Plaintiff such compensatory damages as it sees fit for the suffering, mental anguish, emotional distress, annoyance, loss of time to carry out his fiduciary corporate duties and overall unnecessary inconvenience brought about by the Defendants' illegal activities.

6) A trial by jury.

7) For any further general relief that the court deems proper and just.

Joel Rosenthal, pro se

_____

Point of View Farm, Inc.
HC 64 Box 136A
Hillsboro, WV 24946
304 653 4766

CERTIFICATE OF SERVICE

Copies of this summons were sent to each of the Defendants via Registered Mail on:

Frank Jezioro_____

Mike Pizzino_____

Howard Shinaberry_____

Shane Duffield_____

William Valentino_____

Chapter 25

For a holy endeavor is now to begin
And virtue shall triumph at last

THE FIRM AND THE FEDERAL COURT

In my mind, this case would go before a judge in Charleston where the courts more often than not protected the government rather than upheld the rights of a citizen. If possible, I hoped that I could keep the pressure on Valentino and the DNR a little longer. Because I alleged that my constitutional and civil rights had been violated, I was already thinking that I might be able to then appeal to the federal court and perhaps after that to the U.S. Supreme Court if necessary.

In hindsight, most of what unfolded made sense.

Because a part of my lawsuit requested compensation for damages, the DNR and the Attorney Generals' office turned to their insurer for protection. The infamous AIG had written the liability policy for the WV government. Instead of addressing the issues I raised directly, AIG hired Bailey and Wyant, a large law firm in Charleston to defend these state employees against me.

The firm employs about 30 attorneys and touts itself as being "West Virginia's Insurance Defense Lawyers." My case was to be handled by Charles Bailey and Brian Morrison. Almost all of the correspondence occurred between Brian and me.

To my amazement and delight Brian moved my case from the Circuit Court in Charleston to the Federal Court in Wheeling, West Virginia. This was done because of the Constitutional issues I raised.

So, I was at least out of the clutches of the West Virginia State court system. In Federal Court I thought I stood a much greater chance for success.

The Honorable, John Preston Bailey, Chief U.S. District judge, no relation to Charles Bailey, was assigned to my case.

Brian responded to my suit with a salvo of paperwork containing his motion for dismissal. This was no surprise to me except for the sheer volume.

He argued that my case had no merit. He alleged that I had violated the Rules of Procedure for suing government officials. He presented many references of prior court decisions. And he attacked my motives. When all was said and done he had filed about 100 pages in his motions for dismissal.

Since I was now a veteran of how lawyers worked, I looked at all this material as a bonus and not something to be feared. As usual I reasoned that the more a bureaucrat or a lawyer says or does the more mistakes he will make. Pedantically, I perused all of Brian's material. Of interest I did find mistakes, but I also found areas of concern for me.

When one wants to file a law suit against a public official there are certain steps that have to be taken. One has to tell that official well in advance of your pending actions. I thought I had done this when I responded to Jezioro's Cease and Desist Order, but I was not one hundred percent sure that I said I was going to sue him at a certain time or in particular way.

Thinking that Judge Bailey might just dismiss my case on this basis I fired off some more e-mails to Jezioro to tell him more specifically that I was going to sue him. If Judge Bailey was going to dismiss my case for this reason he would do so without prejudice meaning that I could re-file once I had followed the appropriate procedures. I wanted to be ahead of the curve so that everyone would know that I was not about to give up. In addition I filed a lengthy response to Brian's motion in an attempt to refute all his reasons for seeking his dismissal.

Of course Frank and Will turned over to Brian any and all correspondence I had sent them. My latest e-mails telling them of my intentions to sue them were no exception. Well, this induced Brian Morrison to make his first big mistake. In an effort to elevate himself as being an erudite lawyer he sent me a scathing and threatening letter.

In it he, in a pejorative manner, tried to lecture me on my responsibility to direct all my correspondence to him and not "his" clients. Should I fail to do this, he threatened and "scolded" me, he would take me before Judge Bailey, have the judge reprimand me and award him, Brian, compensation for his time.

So here we go again, I thought. How dare this TWIT treat me this way, like I was someone far beneath him? And since I was on an offensive drive toward the goal line I was not going to let him get away with his nonsense. I, therefore, fired off the following e-mail to him.

Brian,

Thanks for your response, but I have to question whether you learned anything in law school. The defendants in this case are public officials. They occupy their positions at my behest and are paid with my tax dollars. In essences they are my employees. As a citizen I have a right to petition, communicate and correspond with those officials for any grievance I deem appropriate. In case you are unaware of a document called the U.S. Constitution and its amendments you might just find it and read the first amendment.

No public official can be protected from a citizen's written inquiries. Your letter to me was indeed a threat and I have taken it to be such. If you want to play legal games with me in regards to this then bring it on. I have already won one Supreme Court case against the tyranny of your clients and I will be more than happy to take you on in regards to my rights.

I am not a member of your Esquire club and do not have to dance to your version of the Vienna Waltz. I am a citizen of the United States and of the State of West Virginia. My Email to Frank and Will had to do with a potential future action. Should you not realize this and wish to act on your threats that will be fine. Not only will I win, but I will have the courts reprimand you and reimburse me for my time. I will then file ethics charges against you and have you disbarred from your club.

And then if you need a job I will hire you to clean out my animal cages.

If you read closely my Emails you will see that I described myself as a bulldog in regards to my seeking justice. So if you really want to take me on, then do so. The only way you can win is with a corrupt court.

Hope you are having a pleasant day,

Still your most humble antagonist,

See you in federal court.

Joel Rosenthal

Realizing that I was not going to yield to his storm trooper tactics he quickly sent an e-mail back to me where he tried to apologize by saying he was not threatening me and that we should treat each other with Dignity and Respect. If nothing else, I had won this round of gamesmanship, but I was not about to let go of this quarry so easily. I had to press on a little more so that he knew for sure that he messed with me at his own peril. In regards to my law suit he had sent off some material to Judge Maxwell, who initially had the case before it was passed on to Judge Bailey, but Brian had not sent a copy to me. I used this faux pas to excoriate him legally.

From all these years of dealing with judges and especially lawyers I found it upsetting that they all thought the everyday citizen to be beneath them. They had sworn to uphold the law, yet the law was going to be what they said it was. An air of elitism and arrogance permeated their actions. Yes, I wanted Brian to know that not only did I have rights, but in some ways I had more rights than he did. If I had been a lawyer I could not have addressed him in the manner of this next e-mail.

Brian,

Thanks for finally sending me the material you sent to the Federal Court in Elkins and ultimately to Judge Maxwell. Now I will take you at your word that you put a copy in the mail to me a month ago, but I did not receive anything. In response I will in addition to any filings I send to you I will at the very least also inform you of that post by an Email.

But, as Ronald Reagan would say "there you go again." I am not sure what you learned about ex parte communications, but it is really very simple. If you communicate with the court, ie Judge Maxwell, and I do not receive a copy or email of that same information then this by definition is ex parte.

I appreciate your including remarks about dignity and respect, but Brian prior to your sending me that threatening letter early last month designed to bully and intimidate me I did not know of your existence from Adam. You did not begin our

relationship on a very positive footing of dignity and respect. Now I do not know if you have ever dealt with an opposing party who represented himself, but for sure now you have. And one thing you are going to learn in dealing with me is that you are now facing the aggrieved party first hand. Information is not going to be fed to you via a fellow "fraternity" brother. Information is not going to be glossed over so that everyone can get together afterwards and have mint juleps. I am a bear defending her cubs against all threats and you, Brian, presented yourself as a threat.

Brian, your clients have demonstrated that they care not one lick about the law, about court rulings about the Constitution of the land, about their public responsibilities, about their own oaths of office or about abusing their powers. Your clients, Brian, have no morals, no ethics and no sense of their public duties.

As far as I am concerned, Brian, "your" law firm is but a mirror image of these defendants, a part and parcel of the same. You do not care one iota about any of these above values. Brian, you and the rest of the crew at Bailey and Wyant are in reality nothing more than mercenaries, hired guns who simply bill by the hour and care not one whit about what happens. You have a huge conflict of interest between values and what you do because the bottom line for you is simply a dollar sign followed by a lot of numbers. I run a non-profit corporation, you operate a for profit business.

In light of this Brian, you mother may think that you are a "hero" when you represent such scoundrels as these defendants, but Brian to me you and those in the law firm are nothing more than another group of cowboys.

So Brian, I will embrace your concepts of dignity and respect when you convince Will and Frank to do the right thing, to demonstrate that they, too, respect the law by sending me a letter apologizing for having two conservation officers violate my constitutional rights and for their own actions in violation of their oaths of office. And yes, Brian, I also will embrace your words of dignity and respect when Frank and Will retract that ridiculous "Cease and Desist Order."

Brian I do not know if you are 25 years old or 55 years old, but one thing is for sure I just may turn out to be the best thing that ever happens to your legal career. I am still that bull dog I told you about.

No matter what happens Brian, I have already won, not only the criminal case, but in reality this law suit because those deceitful bureaucrats in Charleston and Elkins now know that they violate the law and my rights at their own jeopardy.

Come visit here Brian and you will see what one guy can do and achieve for the State of West Virginia. Bring your family, especially any kids or grandchildren and they can see the animals I have.

Boy do I hope the judge throws out all your motions and allows us to really litigate this case. I will destroy your clients. I salivate just thinking of having especially Frank and Will on the witness stand. I hope you are in the courtroom when that happens.

Joel

In a way it was too bad that I had to act this way. The term "not gentleman like" comes to mind, but I felt I had to respond to everything just to keep the coyotes at bay. Addressing people like Brian Morrison on what they said and did was necessary just to make sure the balance of power was more or less equal.

A lawsuit in federal court has to satisfy several preexisting steps before it might ever go to trial. Additional motions, additional amendments, continuances and court mandates all drag out the process such that a year or many years could go by before there is resolution.

Most lawsuits, whether in state or federal courts are usually dismissed or settled long before there is any formal trial. The costs for both sides often, also, dictate a curtailment of the proceedings. And just like in all my other legal matters I had a huge advantage even against the coffers of an entire state because my costs were hundreds of times less than an average person would spend on just entertainment. And I can guarantee that I was having more fun than any individual should be allowed to have. The State of West Virginia on the other hand was dolling out hundreds of hours of bureaucrat time and travel, dozens of hours of court time and thousands of hours of diversionary time to deal with me. The costs to the State at this point, were probably in the range of hundreds of thousands of dollars and growing.

A phase of the proceedings that I looked forward to was where each side could submit to their adversaries what are called Admissions, Interrogatories and Stipulations. In essence they are a series of questions designed to force the other party to admit to their indiscretions and/or illegal acts or at the very least give the opposing party fodder to use in court.

The other phase which I relished would be when I could force all these bureaucrats to submit to depositions. Here I could meet some of them for the first time, put them each under oath and ask them questions directly. A court stenographer and a tape recording would preserve all the information which could be used in the courtroom.

Most parties to a lawsuit who know they are guilty of the charges will avoid these later two stages at all costs.

Brian and I for the next month or two exchanged information as we followed the schedule sent to us by Judge Bailey. I made a request for Discovery and Brian sent me all the information I already had. We even had a telephone conference with Judge Bailey. For me it was all fun as I waited for Judge Bailey to make a decision on Brian's motions. This he finally did with a 12 page Memorandum.

Chapter 26

I am I, Don Quixote, the lord of La Mancha
My destiny calls and I go

ADVANTAGE SOLIDIFCATION

The inflection point in calculus is the point on a graph where a line curves such that it changes sign or goes from being concave to convex or visa versa. In life the inflection point might be the point whereby someone goes from being poor to rich or sad to happy, or has an epiphany.

In the legal arena it is the point on which a trial or case turns. This might happen with the discovery of new evidence or the testimony of a witness. Often the inflection point of a case involves a decision by the judge swinging the case from one side to the other.

In November of 2008 Judge Bailey made an important ruling and then sent all the parties of my lawsuit his **MEMORANDUM OPINION AND ORDER** comprising 12 pages.

Judge Bailey began by reviewing the full context of my involvement in the justice system. He then went on to explain that **"Inasmuch as the plaintiff** (this is me) **filed this action pro se this Court is required to construe the pleadings liberally."** Fortunately, with this statement Judge Bailey proclaimed that he would not hold me to the legal standard of having to cross every "T" and dot every "I" as long as my message was clear and legal. Several court decisions were mentioned by Judge Bailey to justify this decision.

The Defendants had motioned for dismissal based on their claim that I, the plaintiff, had not properly informed them of my claims nor properly served them my lawsuit. Judge Bailey acknowledged the deficiency of my actions, but refused to dismiss the case on this basis citing decisions of past courts in this matter and reflecting on the concept that the Defendants were not harmed, nor prejudiced by my errors. His citation included the following from a court decision:

"...If it (my lawsuit) **names them** (the Defendants) **in such terms that every intelligent person understands who is meant, as is the case here, it has fulfilled its purpose; and courts should not put themselves in the position of failing to recognize what is apparent to everyone else."** The Defendant's motion to dismiss on this basis was denied on the grounds that indeed there was a **"sufficiency of process."**

Judge Bailey then addressed the motions to dismiss based on a claim of immunity from prosecution because the defendants were government officials, because they have absolute immunity and because they have qualified immunity. With each motion Judge Bailey not only denied the motion, but asserted that the Defendants were liable to the extent of the West Virginia state's insurance along with personal liability because the claims of the Plaintiff allege violations of his Constitutional rights. **"In addition, an action under 42 U.S.C. Code 1983 is an action against state officers in their individual capacity"** he stated.

Judge Bailey then went on to say:

"In this case, the pleaded facts, taken as true, demonstrate that the defendants violated the plaintiff's constitutional rights. By threatening the plaintiff with prosecution after the Circuit Court of Pocahontas County found that he was legally entitled to carry on his activities in caring for abandoned and needy animals,

the defendants violated the plaintiff's due process rights. Turning to the issue of whether the right was clearly established, the fact that a court of law acting within its jurisdiction had found that the plaintiff was entitled to carry on his activities clearly established that right.

Accordingly, defendants Valentino and Jezioro are not entitled to the protection of qualified immunity."

Brian Morrison, attorney for the defendants, also tried to have my case dismissed by noting that WV code prohibits the State from paying any punitive damages. Judge Bailey took this head on by stating that he was ruling the defendants would be subject to any punitive damage personally.

Another point Brian tried to make was that the Statutes of Limitations had run out. On this point Judge Bailey actually partially agreed. In his ruling he noted that the violations by the DNR officers of my Fourth amendment rights occurred when the officers entered my property illegally in 2005. He therefore dismissed my lawsuit against Mike Pizzino, Shane Duffield and Howard Shinaberry. However, my charges of "malicious prosecution" were not dismissed since the Statutes of Limitation cannot begin until the termination of any actions alleged to be malicious were prosecuted.

There is no doubt that after reading this memorandum I could have hugged Judge Bailey. Not only would Will Valentino, Assistant Attorney General and Frank Jezioro, Director of the West Virginia Department of Natural Resources be on the hook for my lawsuit, but Judge Bailey skewered any defense they might have mounted by declaring the evidence supported a violation of my U.S. Constitutional rights and these two would be personally libel for any damages the court might award me.

In a roundabout way, Judge Bailey was telling these guys that by addressing their own motions for dismissal he had tried, convicted and ruled against them. In addition he was telling them that if this case actually went to trial he would award me damages that Valentino and Jezioro would have to cough up out of their own pockets.

The Honorable Judge Bailey by his Memorandum Opinion and Order definitely put me in the cat bird seat.

At this point the insurance company, AIG, was still paying for the defense of these guys in a case they could not win. So I wondered how much longer they would ante up for a losing cause. Then I wondered how much longer Darrell McGraw, the Attorney General, Frances Hughes or Dawn Warfield, who were lawyers themselves and the supervisors for Will Valentino, would allow Will Valentino to be so embarrassing to himself and their office.

Despite these visions of sugar plums dancing in my head I knew that anything could happen. Many years ago Dick Motta coached the Baltimore Bullets in professional basketball. His team was leading 3 games to 1 in the championship series and needed just one more victory. Earlier a sportscaster had remarked that the other team still had a chance by saying "the opera isn't over till the fat lady sings." Closely repeating this, Motta told the news media when asked if his team had the championship wrapped up that "It ain't over till the fat lady sings."

This became a now oft repeated expression. From my now lengthy experience with the legal system I knew that I had to complete the victory before the "fat lady would sing."

My lawsuit was still on track. I had already completed my list of Interrogatories and Admissions which I wanted Valentino and Jezioro to answer. These I sent to Brian Morrison as a way of keeping up the pressure on all of them.

Chapter 27

And the wild winds of fortune will carry me onward
Oh whither so ever they blow

THE FAT LADY SINGS

I had met Tom Smith of the AG office when he drove to Marlinton in a failed attempt to have Judge Pomponio dismiss my actions against the State officials. There I invited him to visit Point of View Farm and he did. He and his son not only got to see what I did, but I could tell they approved.

So in the fall of 2008 I got a call from Tom stating that "we" had to have a meeting. Knowing full well that I was not going to go to Charleston for any "meeting," I hesitated to even respond to him. Finally, though, I agreed, that a meeting might be helpful, beneficial and revealing. However, I told him that under no circumstances was I going to drive to Charleston. I was very satisfied with my legal position. If he wanted a meeting, I told him, he would have to get an old pickup truck, assemble his delegation and drive the three hours to and through the Greenbrier River to my place.

I would prepare a gourmet meal for them and after eating we could have our "meeting." Without any fanfare he agreed.

Tom arrived as scheduled. We bantered and joked about all my "trials and tribulation" during the meal. Tom helped show my place to those attending. Our "meeting" turned out to be pretty short and to the point. "What did I want?" he asked. "Everything I have asked for," I responded. "OK," he said, "I will write it up and send it to you." I closed the conversation with "great."

Despite all my negative dealings with so many lawyers over the years I, nevertheless, had to give Tom the chance to pull this off.

To his word he drafted a document which was called an **OMNIBUS SETTLEMENT AGREEMENT** and was three pages long.

The document referenced my court cases against the state officials, my lawsuit and my Petition for a Writ of Mandamus. In exchange for signing this agreement I would drop both actions. I would then have a document acknowledging my right to care for any animal in Pocahontas County. In addition the Cease and Desist Order from Frank Jezioro would be withdrawn and the ruling of Judge Pomponio in Circuit Court would be recognized.

Of great interest to me was a statement declaring that Valentino and Jezioro would take no action regarding my business license to operate Point of View Farm. For a long time I suspected that they might find some way to have this business license revoked. After all, if I did not have the license then I would not have any Certificate of Authority. Attempting such an action out of revenge would have been highly illegal. With this agreement, though, I had a statement that indeed these guys had considered trying to tamper with my business license, but would not.

The document contained other minor additions and failed to contain other requirements. Fortunately I did not feel that any of the factors of concern or omissions were the result of Tom trying to take advantage of my lack of legal acumen. With each revision I procrastinated in my response so that I could ruminate on the statements and my options.

For about a couple of months, Tom and I made corrections and additions. At no point did he refuse to add or change any of my suggestions. I changed the limitations where I could obtain animals from only Pocahontas County to the entire state of West Virginia. I argued that my business license was not limited to Pocahontas County so neither should any of my activities. Also, I wanted to make sure that anyone who found an animal in need and wanted to give it to me would not be subject to prosecution by the DNR. The opening statement thus read that the **"agreement was between Joel Rosenthal, Point of View Farm, Inc. its agents and employees and the defendants and the State of West Virginia."**

Tom signed the document on behalf of the DNR and Frank Jezioro initialed it. Dawn Warfield, William Valentino's boss' name was also on the document.

I have to admit that I had many reservations about signing this agreement. I had fought these folks for so long and now I had complete control over them. In much the same way as a long journey provides one with so many experiences so, too, had this quest. Reaching one's destination can then bring about let down. This is the way I felt. By signing the document the journey would be over. But I knew that this journey was only as valuable as the final accomplishment. I signed.

Brian Morrison then filed a final document with Judge Bailey affirming the settlement, but I made sure Judge Bailey got a copy of my agreement. I did not trust Jezioro or the State of West Virginia to fully honor what we signed. I wanted to make sure that if the State violated the agreement I could ask Judge Bailey to reopen the case. Should this ever be necessary I will not hesitate to pick up my lawsuit where I left off.

In order to help assure I would not have trouble with law enforcement I took copies of the agreement to the current prosecutor in Pocahontas County, the sheriff and Howard Shinaberry, the DNR officer.

It was difficult for me to realize that I had actually won. So many times in the past I thought a favorable ruling by the courts meant that I would not be harassed again by the State of West Virginia. So many times the State demonstrated that they would do almost anything to shut down my activities. Never, throughout this time, did I stop helping animals. The deer pictures at the head of each chapter represent just a fraction of the wildlife I assisted during this period. But now I had a document from the State affirming the validity of what I do. It hangs proudly from on the wall of my office and I point to it as a crowning achievement.

EPILOGUE

Reflecting on this entire saga I realized that my journey revealed what is the very best about the justice system in the United States and what is the very worst. For sure I demonstrated that one, little guy without any legal acumen can with dedicated persistence win in the highest courts. But on the other hand this was only possible because so many factors seemed to just fall into place. First and foremost I was fighting for the right to continue the work I was doing. Second I was spurred on by the belief that I met all the conditions of the law and third I "needed" to prove something to myself and to those who wanted to deny me my rights.

Ironically, other intangibles played a huge role. By knowing nothing about the law I was enough of a tyro to think that all I had to do was learn it. In addition I did not have a formal job which would make demands on my time. Also, the Internet was mature enough during these years that I could do almost all my research at my desk.

And the corruption that I saw in the system only spurred me on to fight harder. In all I spent thousands of hours on my case, but my costs in dollars were more for gas to drive back and forth to the courthouse than for fees. And a very important aspect of our justice system lies in the fact that judges are supposed to give some deference to a pro se defendant. Every judge in the higher courts respected my verve and even acknowledged it. I doubt that any real lawyer no matter what he might be paid could have been successful in this situation.

For me my victory was exhilarating, but I also realized that what I endured was a true anomaly. After all I was only facing a misdemeanor conviction and a fifty dollar fine. Most people have jobs and families to care for. Most people, like me, develop pangs of fear when the justice system is even mentioned. Most people are pragmatic and sensible. Most people think that the "system" is stacked against them and would have a difficult time if this fear was confirmed. Even the West Virginia Supreme Court did not understand or acknowledge the illegality of their action or the legality of my own. Only a "crazy" person would spend so many years trying to overturn such an insignificant citation. In the past I, too, have paid as quickly as I could fines for traffic violations just to put the circumstances behind me and get on with my life. The costs for me or anyone else to have hired a lawyer in this case would have run into the hundreds of thousands of dollars and from what I have seen this would only have guaranteed an ultimate defeat.

Lawyers are officers of the court. They are part of the system. None would want a judge to think of him as being illiterate of the law or abusive of the system. In isolated areas like Pocahontas County only a few lawyers handle 90% of the cases. These lawyers are before the same judges over and over and while they will put forth legal arguments, it is rare that they will go out on a limb for anyone. A lawyer's reputation in small town America is far more important than the disposition of a client.

Because of the publicity my cases generated, people from all over the state remembered who I was when they found animals in need of care. These folks were delighted that finally there was someone in West Virginia who could care for wild animals.

Most people in this state still think that the DNR cares about animals in need. Their knee jerk reaction when finding an orphan or injured animal is to call the DNR. If they are lucky they are simply scolded for having picked up the animal and threatened with arrest if they do not immediately throw the animal back into the environment to die. If they are unlucky, like Stoots and Harvey, they are hauled into court and have to pay a stiff fine. And if they are really unlucky the DNR will show up at their home, kill the animal right in front of them and then arrest them.

Little by little though some bureaucrats have seen the importance of what I do. Several attorneys from the Attorney Generals' office have now visited my facility. Tony Tatano, my old, adversarial, assistant, prosecuting attorney has been here a few times. The last time he brought me an injured owl. Even throughout my legal odyssey and when I have thrown scathing vituperations at government and law firm officials I have still extended invitations to all of them to visit.

I have had hundreds of other guests from all over the world. Not one has voiced a negative comment about the mission and actions of what I do here at Point of View Farm. Many of the new visitors have told me that they have wanted to visit ever since one of their friends had told them about my place.

Spring is usually the busiest time for me. This is when most baby animals are born, raised and introduced to the world. Probably the largest number of orphans occurs when mothers are killed while trying to cross a highway with their young. All will perish if not detected and rescued by some Good Samaritan and brought to me.

What I do is in reality such a small, insignificant fraction of what happens in nature. Charles Darwin's Survival of the Fittest is not a misnomer. Mother Nature is brutal. She takes no prisoners. Any compromise to the health and welfare of an animal in the wild, results in death. And all but the animals at the top of the food chain either are predatory on others or are eaten themselves. Even the animals at the top of the food chain, should they suffer injuries, a dearth of available food or even changes in the weather, can starve and expire quickly. And then they all are subject to deadly organisms and parasites. Even the animals I raise and release are not immune to these ravages. Those that "hang" around I feed, but those who vanish into the wilderness simply blend into what nature has to offer. Sometimes, and more often than I would hope, animals die under my care. Every such situation is devastating, but understandable. No matter what, it seems that I have to just keep plugging along.

With all of this being said, the rewards for me are incalculable. I imagine somewhere in my genetic code lies a fragment of DNA that programs me to have a maternal inclination. With compromised animals, I often care for them by putting them under my shirt and against the depression between my chest and stomach. For hours or even days they are secure here next to the warmth of my body and with the rhythm of my heart and breathing. Quite often I have found that this can make the difference between life and death.

Of course the animals give back to me much more than I do for them. I am a biologist and scientist by training and by avocation. Trying to understand the world around us is what makes me tick. Every animal has its own unique mechanism and behavior of how to live. Humans have asked questions about why any animal does what it does ever since our brains evolved to be big enough to ponder. After all, early humans not only foraged for food, but hunted to survive. By my being able to interact so intimately with wildlife, these animals tell me by their actions and instincts what they are all about. In the process I learn something about what makes them "tick."

Occasionally, an animal I raised and released will maintain the capacity to blend seamlessly between being completely "wild" and yet maintain a relationship with me. These individuals on their own, avoid other humans, but do emerge from the wilderness to make contact with me. When I lived in suburbia this very relationship occurred with a skunk, a fox, crows, an opossum and raccoons. Despite my proximity to neighbors, these animals were invisible to other humans, but often revisited my house. Here in the mountains I have no neighbors on my side of the river for miles. Most animals have a home territory much smaller than this.

It is impossible to describe the overall ambiance created when a wild animal comes out of the forest to interact with me. Currently, a deer, I call Blossom, that I raised almost 8 years ago will, when she sees me, come from the fields or forest for a hug and of course for a treat. This she does whether or not I give her any food, but I am not so naïve to think that she does this simply because she "loves" me. And, Rose, a black bear I raised, will occasionally show up. When this happens she and I will go for a hike around the farm. She still thinks of me as her mother. If I get down on the ground with her she will still try to nurse. In the late fall I take the opportunity of her visits to put her in an enclosure during bear hunting season to protect her. Here she makes a den. During this time we still go for our hikes, but she returns on her own back to her den. On one occasion when we got about a half a mile from her enclosure she took off and sprinted the entire way back. When the weather finally warms she chooses once again to live in the forest.

Point of View Farm is the most wonderful place east of the Rocky Mountains. When I pick up visitors on the "other" side of the river I tell them that just like John Denver sang, most of West Virginia is "Almost Heaven," but when they cross the Greenbrier River and visit Point of View Farm there is no "Almost" about my place. I proclaim that they will be entering Nirvana and that they never again will have to wonder what Heaven is all about.

POST SCRIPT

Most of the participants in my case have moved on.

Shane Duffield works for the West Virginia National Guard.
Capt. Mike Pizzino retired from the DNR.
Walt Weiford retired as Pocahontas County Prosecutor.
Doshia Webb, Pocahontas County Magistrate, quit to run for sheriff and lost.
I lost track of Shane Harvey and James Stoots
Pete Treadway died in 2010
Judge Jolliffe, Chief 11th Circuit Court Judge, retired.
Tom Smith retired from the Attorneys Generals' office.
William Valentino remains an Assistant Attorney General
Frank Jezioro, while still Director of the DNR, has spoken of retirement.
Brian Morrison still works for Bailey and Wyant
Howard Shinaberry, Conservation Officer, talks of retirement
Supreme Court Justice Brent D. Benjamin remains on the bench
Supreme Court Justice Robin Jean Davis remains on the bench
Supreme Court Justice Joseph Albright died in 2009
Supreme Court Justice Elliott "Spike" Maynard lost reelection in 2008
Supreme Court Justice Larry Starcher did not run for reelection in 2008 .
Judge Joseph Pomponio, Jr. 11th Circuit Court Judge remains on the bench
Federal Judge John Preston Bailey remains on the bench.

Tony Tatano, Pocahontas County Assistant Prosecutor, was disbarred in 2008 after receiving a criminal conviction for using client's funds for his personal use.

Tony Tatano, 48 was arrested March 16, 2012 on charges of three counts of abandoning an animal, three counts withholding proper sustenance from animals and two counts no rabies vaccine. Bond was set at $2,000. Tatano also pleaded no contest to a charge of worthless check complaint. He was assessed a $1 fine, $160.80 in court costs, $25 worthless check fee, $25 arrest fee and ordered to pay $100 in restitution. A second charge of worthless check complaint was dismissed and he was assessed a $25 worthless check fee and ordered to pay $100 in restitution..

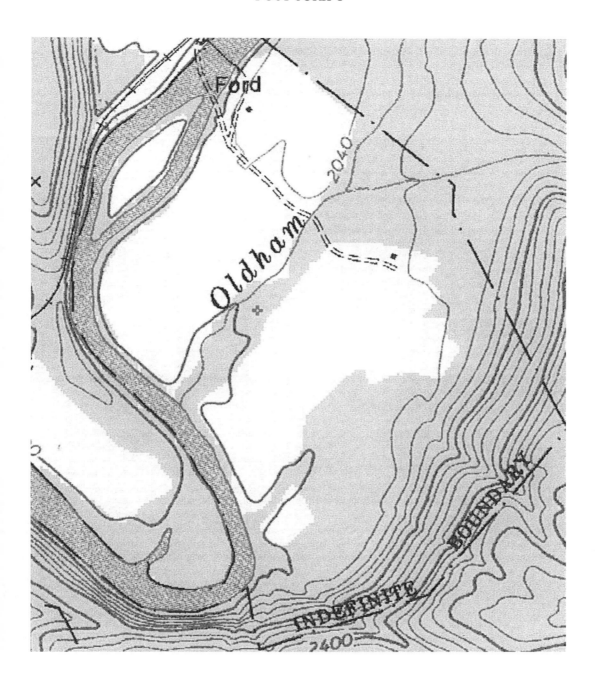

POV FARM

Inside the boundary